You *Will* Be Satisfied

You *Will* Be Satisfied

Ford Motor's top salesman shows you
how to turn happy customers
into fanatical loyalists and leave your
competitors in the dust . . .

Bob Tasca
with Peter Caldwell

HarperBusiness
A Division of HarperCollinsPublishers

HarperCollins books may be purchased for educational, business, or sales promotional use. For information please write: Special Markets Department, Harper Collins Publishers, Inc., 10 East 53rd Street, New York, NY 10022.

FIRST EDITION

Designed by C. Linda Dingler

Library of Congress Cataloging-in-Publication Data

Tasca, Bob.
    You *will* be satisfied / Bob Tasca with Peter Caldwell. — 1st ed.
      p. cm.
    ISBN 0-88730-798-1
    1. Consumer satisfaction.   2. Success in business.   I. Caldwell, Peter.
  II. Title.
  HF5415.335.T37   1996
  658.8'12—dc20   96-3983

96 97 98 99 00 ❖/HC 10 9 8 7 6 5 4 3 2 1

Contents

PART I:
Business Fundamentals:
What Kind of Business Do You Want to Run?

PART II:
The New Job 1:
Creating Satisfied Customers

Foreword

Over the many years of my auto industry involvement, I've heard legend after legend about the individual car dealers who've left their mark on the local market they've served. Some imprints were positive, some negative; but each legend was based in some individual's style or mode of operation. The majority of the nation's car dealers no longer possesses the stuff of legendary appeal. The dealers are becoming nameless corporate business suits. The illustrious car dealers, like the heroes of the Old West, are fast dying out as the world around them changes dramatically and forever. In the 1950s, when Bob Tasca started running a car dealership, he joined nearly fifty thousand entrepreneurs in the United States doing the same thing. Since then, while the industry's unit sales volume has approximately doubled—from 7.5 million to 15 million new vehicles sold annually—the number of entrepreneurs has declined to less than fifteen thousand.

As the entrepreneurial car dealer ranks thin, I try to meet and spend time with as many of those disappearing legends as I can, to learn what makes them tick. Bob Tasca was one of those fabled industry entrepreneurs whom I never seemed to encounter in my many travels, until one day about ten years ago after our company was retained by the Ford Motor Company to conduct a series of focus groups composed of a cross section of its dealership body. Ford wanted to get some in-depth feedback on how its dealers felt about its new policies (which had been instituted to make the auto giant more sensitive to its end customers, the car buyers, and to its intermediaries, the dealerships). In one of those focus groups, there he was, seemingly bigger than life. Sometimes you really have to work hard in a focus group to get participant responses; you really have to dig. In this session, Bob simply took over and spent the next three hours telling all of us what "the Bible according to Bob" said about customer care. It was really quite a stunning performance. As focus-group research, it was a blowout, but as an educational experience it was superb.

As I read Bob's book today, I can't help thinking back to that initial meeting, which Bob totally dominated. I'm hard-pressed to think of a single car dealer practitioner who eats, sleeps, and breathes his business philosophy as convincingly as Bob Tasca. His personal beliefs have been the key to his success—to what he has accomplished in the past forty years at his Ford and Lincoln-Mercury dealerships in southern New England, perhaps one of the toughest auto markets in the United States.

I couldn't agree more with Bob's views on running a business, as I heard them ten years ago and as I read them now—especially a business as difficult as automotive retailing. He's made a lot of money and kept his customers happy—and that's really saying something in the auto business. I'm certain there are other fields where he could have done even better.

In *You* Will *Be Satisfied*, Bob outlines his principles for success in an anecdotal and entertaining manner, with a serious message communicated behind the enjoyable stories. The book is an important primer for young or old who want to be successful business people in a tougher and tougher competitive environment.

When Bob gives his reasons for writing the book, he lets us in on such secrets as: "Knowing my business principles is, in a sense, the easier part of the problem; practicing what I preach is the tougher part." He goes on to say, "Once you've got the business agenda right, then it's all execution." He explains that success has to come from within you—not from getting lucky out there. Once you set your agenda, it's how you treat your employees and, in turn, how your employees treat your customers that determine your success. If you can satisfy the customer, then success and money follow—not the other way around.

—J. D. Power III
President
J.D. Power and Associates
December 1995

The Blue Ribbon Award:
A Dedication Story

Thanks to my family—past, present, and future. Most immediately, to my grandson Carl who cared enough about his school to inspire me to help keep it open and to a remarkable school principal who cared enough to make it happen.

My seven-year-old grandson Carl came home from school one day and said to me with tears in his eyes, "Poppy, they're going to close my school."

I said to him, "Carl, do you really care about your school?"

He said, "Poppy, I *love* my school."

"Well then," I said, "it won't close."

I went to see the pastor, and I said, "If I can make the school an asset—rather than a liability—to the parish, will you keep it open?" He agreed.

Subsequently, I discovered that the school had many liabilities and an enrollment that had dropped from a high of more than 500 to only about 250; the reality looked pretty grim. But I also learned that the school had one asset that shone like a newly minted silver dollar: Sister Mary Carol Gentile, the new principal. I knew at once that she had the rare gift of entrepreneurship; she'd be a huge business success if she weren't working for the Lord. He got her first.

I decided that the school needed two things: an improved product and some good marketing. So, first of all, we determined what was wrong with the product, then we fixed it, and then we told the world about it. In other words, we used the same principles I'm about to describe in this book.

How did we determine what was wrong? Well, my coauthor, Peter Caldwell, who was teaching marketing at Providence College, suggested we do focus-group research, and together with Marty Goldfarb Associates we ran a series of focus groups that told us what needed fixing. Then, Sister Mary Carol did what needed doing.

How did we tell the world about it? Well, Sister Mary Carol led an effort that got the school a national Blue Ribbon Award for Excellence in education three years later. That allowed us to tell a wonderful story: When you enroll your child at St. Rocco's, you're enrolling him or her at a National Blue Ribbon school.

In other words, Sister bet on the come: She bet that the opportunity to get that award would so challenge the school that together, as a team, the teachers, students, and parents could do it. And they did. It was a real rags-to-riches story, financially and educationally. Enrollment took off, the huge deficits disappeared, and the educational program improved immensely—all at the same time.

Last fall, I took Sister Mary Carol and two of her teachers down to Washington to celebrate and to receive the award from the president. Only three people from St. Rocco's could go to the ceremony. Sister Mary Carol wanted me to go, but I said no; I told her the people who'd done the most to earn the award should go and shake hands with the president. And they did.

Today, I can say without a doubt that St. Rocco's School in Johnston, Rhode Island, is one of the finest primary-middle schools anywhere. We're going to make it even better, by building a "team center" that teaches athletics, applied science, and healthy cooperative values in team play all at the same time. Then, we'll share our program with other schools.

I agreed to write this book to help make the team center happen financially. When you buy *You Will Be Satisfied*, you'll be helping to create a future revolution in education. You might wonder about this and ask, "Tasca, if you're so successful, why don't you just *give* the school the money?" Well, I could do that—but then I'd be violating a principle I've been teaching all my children and grandchildren: When you want something, you have to *earn* it.

So, at age sixty-nine, I'm learning to be an author so that I can earn my school a new team center. Do you know what? I'm having a wonderful time at my new profession.

Introduction:
The Fat Mechanic Out Back

A True Customer Satisfaction Story

One Saturday afternoon during the early fall of 1957, I was busy doing repairs on a customer's car. I'd opened my Ford dealership, Tasca Ford, three years before at the ripe young age of twenty-seven. From the beginning, I'd known what kind of business I wanted to run: one focused on selling and servicing automobiles—one that would give customers satisfaction as they'd never dreamed of before. It wasn't long after I'd started the business that I'd committed to evening and weekend service. Nobody else anywhere offered that back then; it was unheard of—but I knew I had to do it to make my customers happy. At first, my people balked at working evenings and on Saturdays; they changed their minds, though, when I told them we'd have extended-hours service within a month or I'd padlock the doors and go out of business. I felt that strongly about it. They believed me, and after a while, they discovered it wasn't so bad after all. *Making your customers happy has its own rewards.* So, there I was that Saturday afternoon, replacing a water pump so a customer could have his car for the remainder of the weekend.

When I started my dealership, I was the mechanic as well as salesman and general manager; in fact, I was the only full-time employee. By 1957, my business had grown much bigger; we'd relocated three times, most recently into a large, brand-new facility on 777 Taunton Avenue in East Providence, Rhode Island. Within five years "777" would become the second largest Ford dealership in the world. But this was still 1957, and even though I now employed a number of mechanics, I still worked on customer cars myself. I've always worked harder than anybody else, and this was one of my Saturdays on duty. So, there I was.

I remember the day very well; it was one of those clear, hot, summerlike September days that anyone who's lived in New England knows very well—a day that, had it occurred earlier in the year, would probably have sent everyone to the beaches. It was so hot that the tarmac outside the service area had turned soft, and you could see the heat waves rising off it. As I wiped the sweat from my forehead, I looked up to see a brand-new car swing into the dealership, still going fast, tires squealing, billows of white smoke pouring out from underneath the hood.

The driver brought the car to a sudden halt near the car I was working on, and I knew at once that he had to be some Ford bigwig. The car was an experimental job, and only a Ford executive would have such a car. I was pretty sure this particular vehicle was a preproduction Edsel—Ford's soon-to-be-released big new entry into the mid-priced field for 1958.

The guy got out and came over to me. "Boy, I'm lucky to find you here on a Saturday. My car's overheated, and I need to get to a wedding this weekend on Cape Cod. I'm already late. Can you fix it?"

Everything about him communicated impatience; he was a man in a hurry—a man used to giving orders.

Well, I could see right away without even lifting the hood that the problem wouldn't be easily solved. I confirmed that the car was a preproduction Edsel, which meant I couldn't just change some parts; I wouldn't even have them. "I *can* fix it for you," I said, "but I can't have it for you today. I'll tell you what I can do for you, though. Give me the address where you're going to be on the Cape, and you take my car. I'll fix your car and deliver it to you tomorrow morning. Then we can swap back."

"You'll do all that?" he asked.

"Sure," I said.

So, the guy drove off in my Ford demonstrator. I didn't even get his name. I wasn't worried, though—after all, his car was worth a lot more than mine!

Early Sunday morning, I asked my wife if she'd like to drive to the Cape for the day. She said sure, so we got into the Ford executive's experimental car and drove to one of those large Cape Cod estates. The gatekeeper told me where on the estate the guy had left my car. I'd brought an extra set of keys, so I just left his car and took my own. We went on our way to morning Mass and then enjoyed the Cape for the day. Then we drove back home. I thought nothing more about it. Arranging "swaps" was just something I did for my customers.

About a week later, when I was opening the day's business mail, I came across an official-looking letter on Ford Motor Company stationery addressed to "Robert F. Tasca Sr., President, Tasca Ford." The letter read something like this:

> *Dear Mr. Tasca:*
>
> I had occasion last Saturday to stop at your dealership in East Providence, Rhode Island. My car had overheated and needed repairing. Never in my forty years in the automobile business have I ever encountered such an extraordinary example of customer service as I did at your dealership that day. [The letter went on to recount the details of the customer service incident.]
>
> I wish to most heartily congratulate you on the very fine dealership organization you run. Incidentally, please give my thanks to the fat mechanic out back.
>
> > *Sincerely,*
> > *Ernest Breech*
> > *Chairman*

I leaned back in my chair and laughed. The "fat mechanic out back" had been me, of course. Well, at the next national dealership convention in New York City, who do you think wanted to talk with me? Ernie Breech, of course. And he wanted me to meet "the Deuce"—Henry Ford II. People often ask how I came to be so influential with Ford's top brass. Well, that's how it all began. I did it by satisfying a customer—a guy who'd never bought a car from me and obviously never would. A guy I never expected to see again. I hadn't cared; I'd satisfied him anyhow.

The Juggernaut in Seekonk

I'd pity anyone who wanted to be my competitor. I'd feel sorry for anyone trying to compete with that Juggernaut out in Seekonk. Why, we'd just kill him. He wouldn't stand a chance. He'd be bankrupt within six months.

—BOB TASCA SR.

Some people in the Providence, Rhode Island, area believe I don't have any local competitors selling Lincolns and Mercurys because I have a sweetheart deal with the Ford Motor Company or with the Ford family. This "competition issue" came up one night when I participated in a business school class at Providence College. One of the students asked me if I had any competitors. I said no—that I used to have six, but they all went out of business. Then he asked me what would happen if a competitor opened up in my sales area. I knew what he was getting at—that my success was based on an unfair advantage I'd secured through Ford. I told him that I'd feel real sorry for my competitor. The Juggernaut out in Seekonk (Tasca Lincoln-Mercury, located in Seekonk, Massachusetts, right near Providence) would just steamroller him. We'd kill him. He'd be bankrupt in six months. The reason that I don't have any competitors is that my reputation for customer satisfaction is so widespread nobody in my trading area would want to buy a Lincoln or a Mercury from anyone else.

Tasca Lincoln-Mercury has reached a very enviable position in the metropolitan Providence area: We regularly capture 12 to 16 percent of the *total* new car market. Lincoln-Mercury nationally does only about 4 to 6 percent. We have outsold all seven area Ford dealers combined. Other dealers ask, "Seekonk where?" They can't believe that a leading dealership could be located in tiny, little, out-of-the-way Seekonk.

Why do we outsell Lincoln-Mercury nationally by about four to one? It's entirely due to our total customer satisfaction business agenda. Incidentally, we don't just dominate when times are good. During the last recession, our share reached as high as 24 percent: We were selling nearly one out of every four new cars in a metropolitan area populated by more than three-quarters of a million people. When times are good in the auto business, almost anybody can sell cars and make money. I wouldn't say we're recession-proof, but we excel when times are bad. That is, during hard times we may drop a bit in sales, but other dealerships go in the bag; some of them go bankrupt.

The Juggernaut in Seekonk actually became a reality in April 1971. That's when Lee Iacocca personally asked me if I would consider opening a Lincoln-Mercury dealership in Seekonk (just over the state line into Massachusetts)—even if it were on an interim basis. He wanted to put Lincoln-Mercury on the map in the Providence area. I agreed to take on the Seekonk store, providing Ford bought me out of the store just up the road. By then, we'd built up 777 to a sales level that ranked it as the second-largest Ford dealership in the world. We sold seven thousand new and used units a year.

At the time, people thought I was nuts to want to sell the Ford store, since it was so successful. But I had my reasons. I didn't want my sons who were coming into the business to have people say, "Your old man built this, and he gave it to you. That's why you're successful." I wanted them to *earn* success—and they have. And I wanted to start over so that I could perfect my customer satisfaction approach. There were a lot of things I'd had to compromise on at the Ford store, and this time, I wanted to get it right.

I guess I was also attracted by the challenge of building another success. I thought, let's try it again. It was probably my ego talking, but I said to myself, "Bob, you've been to the Superbowl (number one or two in sales volume worldwide) once. Do it again and people will think more of you." Lincoln-Mercury has become the Tasca family's second Superbowl: Since 1986, we've won the Ford Motor Company's Chairman's Award for highest customer satisfaction rating nine times in a row. We're consistently among the top ten dealers in sales; and in 1986, we ranked number one in sales for the first time. That year, we sold 3,664 new cars, all out of a facility designed to do just 390! They say that if you do it three times the fans will *love* you. Well, we haven't yet done it three times, but you know something? We'll go to the Superbowl again, because what we do today works.

I opened the Lincoln-Mercury store on October 1, 1971. Ford capitalized it as a company store at $177,400 on the books. They designed it as a 390-unit store—that is, the building and the car lots were designed to sell 390 new cars a year and service the resulting customer base. They asked me how I wanted to be paid, and I said compensation wasn't important. I suggested I take a small salary and just let my share of the profits accrue, so that I could own the store by buying it out. That was all right with Ford management. They figured the store would lose money for the first two to three years anyhow, and then I'd start to accrue money toward the buyout. They figured the buyout would be a long way off.

Where Are All the Cars?

—Carl Tasca

In 1986, the year we first achieved number one in Lincoln-Mercury sales worldwide, we got into a hell of a sales race with a large dealership in Texas. Right down to the year's end, it was neck and neck. We did *everything* we possibly could to sell more cars. On New Year's Eve, it was all over. We went home exhausted. We wouldn't know for several days yet that we'd actually beaten out the other guy and were number one with 3,664 new cars sold.

A few nights later, someone from the Texas dealership showed up and offered our security guard money to let him in to check our sales numbers. The guy got into our lot, and he looked around. Empty. He said to the guard, "Where are all the cars?"

The guard answered, "We sold them."

I think right then and there the guys from Texas learned they'd lost, and to an upstart from little old Rhode Island.

The Lincoln-Mercury store made money from the first month it opened—October 1971—even with all the write-offs and start-up expenses. In fact, I couldn't put any more start-up expenses into the statement that month. I wanted to just clear the air, so that starting in November I wouldn't have any extraordinary expenses to charge.

The Ford controller for my area came down to check me out. He couldn't believe what had happened. Incidentally, Tasca Lincoln-Mercury has never had a red month. Instead of losing money the first three years, it made money from the first day. By the time July 1972 rolled around, I was able, out of my share of the profits, to take over the store. So you could literally say that I didn't buy the store, I earned it—and in less than eight months.

Lincoln-Mercury Division at that time wasn't doing so well nationally. In Providence, it was doing terribly; the division had about 0.8 of 1 percent of the market, which meant that about 1 out of every 120 cars sold was a Lincoln or Mercury. Lincoln-Mercury was a total failure in this market. In fact, it was their lowest-penetration market in the country; they sold fewer cars as a percentage of the market in the Providence metropolitan area than they did anywhere else. I thought it would be a lot of fun building it up. Obviously, I couldn't lose. Lincoln-Mercury's rank couldn't go down; it had to go up. In Providence, division management had changed eleven dealers in fifteen years. The division had six franchised dealerships, and none of them was making any money. In the six previous months, I think they'd sold one new Lincoln between them!

In our first year, we sold about six or seven hundred new cars, considerably more than the volume the store had been designed for. But, for the first three years, the Lincoln-Mercury store wasn't really a boomer. I kept it a fairly small operation until my sons began to come into the business in 1974 through 1979. In fact, I had an agreement with Ford management that I wouldn't muddy the waters right away and start competing with the other dealers to the point at which I started taking a lot of business away from them.

We stayed at about eight or nine hundred units the second year, and then twelve or thirteen hundred the third. Then we coasted at about fourteen hundred through the 1970s. Our big sales growth came in the 1980s when we started doing more than three thousand new cars annually through the "Pre-Trade Plan" and other programs. (I'll tell you more about those later.) We now gross more than sixty million dollars out of one small store designed to do about fifteen million in today's dollars.

From the beginning, I wanted to make the Lincoln-Mercury

store a model dealership from the standpoint of customer satisfaction. Happily, I could start from scratch and institute innovative pricing policies, change pay plans, and focus on customer satisfaction to a much greater extent than I was able to do at the Ford store. This time around, knowing more about what I was doing, I could hire a slightly different kind of person and train people the right way.

Starting in 1971, we actually put into place a philosophy I'd been preaching since the 1950s: one-price selling. For years I'd wanted to "menu-price" the cars I sold—sell every car of the same model at the same price. That way, every customer would pay the same dollars for the same product, and a lot of the horse-trading practices that have hurt the industry would go away.

I'd had some success with menu-pricing customized products in the sixties. In 1960 for instance, Tasca Ford introduced the world's first vinyl-topped car, a customized version of the Falcon. We sold our custom models at a single price, a menu price. They were one-price cars, because they were different. Nobody else had them.

But you see, until you establish a reputation for customer satisfaction, customers in my industry will go looking for a better price elsewhere. And building a track record doesn't happen overnight. Our integrity didn't become the deciding factor the first year or the second year, or even the first five or ten years. It took decades before we could sit in the position we're in today, where every new car with the same equipment sells at the same price.

Today I can make a flat statement: You cannot beat the Tasca family with price. The only way you can beat the Tasca family is to be *better* than we are, and that's tough. In this book, I'm going to tell you something about the principles we've used to get to this position, so you, too, can get off the price competition merry-go-round.

And don't let the long time period discourage you! It may have taken me twenty years to achieve total integrity, but you can make much progress in as little as a year. After all, I'm an ultra-perfectionist. The important thing to understand is that customer satisfaction is not a destination, *it's a continual journey*. If you haven't already, you need to get started on that journey in your business now.

Ford has spent a lot of money over the years trying to figure out what makes my stores tick. We tend not to follow the customary rules. Back in 1986, Ford sponsored a survey in Providence and asked the question, "If you could buy the new car of your choice from any dealer, who would you choose?" Tasca was selected by 84.6 percent of the people interviewed. That's a very revealing figure, because an overwhelming majority of these people hadn't bought a new car from Tasca. Obviously, Lincoln-Mercury products don't sell 84.6 percent of the market. Clearly, their high opinion of Tasca derived from word of mouth.

There are people who would like to buy from Tasca who won't, because Tasca doesn't have the product they want. That's the reason we have about 15 percent of the market instead of 85 percent of the market. But they do want to buy Tasca. *Tasca*, in a sense, is stronger than the product. So Tasca could sell anything and be successful. Today, when people buy from us, they don't buy a Ford or a Lincoln or a Mercury; they buy Tasca. That's the difference. I wonder how many other retailers can make that statement?

We really don't have to depend on the factory having the best vehicle in the marketplace year after year—that's virtually impossible. Nobody bends the metal right consistently. Nobody has the right power train combinations every year. There is no one manufacturer who can say, "We're head and shoulders above everybody else." Incidentally, that's true for many industries—not just the auto industry. Look at computers or photocopiers; do IBM and Xerox have an overwhelming advantage? In this very competitive market today, they're all good. Some of them are better, but they're all good. So no one manufacturer has a corner on anything. That's why customer satisfaction, what everybody today preaches about, is all important.

Of course, it's a lot easier to preach customer satisfaction than it is to know how to make it happen—or to practice it.

A major factor in the automobile business is repeats. Is there a difference between a satisfied customer repeating and a nonsatisfied customer repeating? As you might expect, there is a vast difference. Our customer loyalty rating (defined as actual repeat purchasing behavior) is about 65 percent year after year (the only reason it isn't higher is that some people simply want a change; they want to drive a different car). By contrast, the average new car dealership has a loyalty rating under 20 percent. That pretty much says it all. There is a difference between happiness and unhappiness—and it's about 80 percent.

Does the repeat rule for success hold for all businesses? Pretty much so. There *are* a few businesses where the key to success doesn't lie in making customers for life. But think about it, *does a diamond have to be "forever"?* If you as a jeweler could change your customers' *thinking* and *feeling* about a diamond and its setting, you could sell the same customer several anniversary rings over a lifetime—each time moving up in value. What's the important principle in this case? *Creating a trading cycle where there isn't one now.*

The Great Experiment

I didn't know it at the time, but when I sold my Ford franchise back to the Ford Motor Company, a great experiment in business philosophies began. When I left 777 Taunton Avenue, that dealership was the most successful Ford dealership in the world; all the new owners had to do was to continue my success formula based in customer satisfaction. I even left almost all the workers there. Instead, the new management changed the business agenda. They thought they knew better. And while my Lincoln-Mercury dealership just down the road in Seekonk went from nothing to number one under *my* business agenda, 777 went from number one to bankruptcy under the traditional business person's agenda.

What makes this turn of events even stranger is that my business practices have never been a secret; I've regularly run seminars for Ford Motor Company dealers since the late 1950s. What I've done has been an open book. Hence, the operators of 777 could have easily followed my formula. They chose not to, though, and the results speak for themselves.

The second part of the great experiment began in the summer of 1994 when I agreed to once more run the 777 store. We opened a remodeled store in October 1994. When it had folded, 777 had been last in customer satisfaction ratings and among the lowest in unit sales for the seven Providence-area Ford dealers. Eight months later, in June 1995, we'd built the Ford store up so that it ranked number one in customer satisfaction and number two in sales volume. We're well on our way to our third Superbowl.

How have we done it? The building is the same, except for some badly needed refurbishing (the previous owners hadn't made the investment to keep it updated). Many of the people are the same; we didn't dismiss anybody. We took on all the salespeople from the previous operation who wanted to work for us, and we're retraining them in our philosophy and practices. We still have some of the same service technicians as well. What *has* changed is the business agenda, along with the supporting business practices. We apply the same principles we invented and fine-tuned over the years, first at the original 777 and then at the Juggernaut in Seekonk.

It will be a while until we're as successful at 777 as at Seekonk; it will take time to build up the repeat customer base we have at the other store. But I feel confident in making two predictions: First, that 777 will eventually rank number one in customer satisfaction worldwide for Ford dealerships, just as the Juggernaut in Seekonk ranks number one for Lincoln-Mercury dealerships. And second, the future of American automobile dealerships has been pretty much baked right here in Providence, Rhode Island. Generally speaking, business people—in any industry—who don't adopt our customer satisfaction business agenda will find themselves increasingly unable to compete in tomorrow's marketplace.

Why I'm Not a Mega-Dealer

Until recently, I never ran more than one retail location. Even now, we own only two, and we don't plan to have any more. Partly, I agreed to take back the Ford store so that the next generation of Tascas would have room to grow in the business. People often ask me why I'm not a mega-dealer, selling a number of competing makes of automobiles and operating a number of stores. In fact, *business people today all too often believe that operating a chain, or being a part of a chain, is the only way to business success.* They think bigness itself is the answer, whether it's in manufacturing or retailing. I think I'm living proof that that's not so.

You can always compete successfully against the big chains, or bigger manufacturers—if you have something unique to offer, and you satisfy your customers. You know, I just love neat, clean, bright stores that are *small*. I love small manufacturing businesses. Over the years, I've made as much money, or more, running one store than most people have made running a number of stores. And I've done it not by trying to make a lot of money, but by satisfying my customers.

I'm not a mega-dealer, first, because of my customer satisfaction principles. If I sold several competing makes of automobile, then when my customers asked me which one was best, I'd have to tell them—and the management of the other makes wouldn't like that. You see, I don't sell cars strictly to make a lot of money. I sell cars because I like selling cars. If I don't like a car model, I won't sell it. There've been some Ford Motor Company products over the years I've refused to sell, until certain things were made right in them.

Let's say, for instance, that I'm a mega-dealer and I have ten product offerings. Let's say you came to me to buy a new vehicle and you asked me, "Bob, which one is best?" I'd have to tell you. I'd sell you one of the ten; obviously, I wouldn't sell you the other nine. As a result, I would be very successful with the brands I think are best for you and very much a failure with the ones I don't think are best for you. So, as a result, I wouldn't be a very good dealer across the board.

I'm also not a mega-dealer because I like being close to my customers. I'm not an ivory tower executive. I don't closet myself away. I've never had a secretary. I take all my phone calls; I don't have them screened. I've never refused to call someone back. Maybe that's crazy. Maybe I'd be a colossal failure as a chief executive of a larger company where you have to delegate more. Maybe that's the reason I never worked for a larger company: I like to be on the front lines. At Tasca Ford or Lincoln-Mercury, my customers know that they can always come to me with a problem if they're not satisfied, and I'll take care of them. Of course, knowing my customers enables me to take chances with product—what I call *betting on the come*—with a much greater likelihood of success; I *know* what my customers want.

I'm also not a mega-dealer because I believe in commitment. The multiple-makes dealership game can become like quick marriage and divorce. Marriages of convenience always end up that way. The product line I take on today will likely become the dog that I drop tomorrow, if all I'm in business for is a quick profit.

I've been with the Ford Motor Company for more than fifty years. I'm going to stick with the Ford Motor Company until death do us part. (I've also been married for over forty-five years, and to the same woman.) Sure, there've been times when Ford hasn't had the best products, though fortunately that's not true now. I stuck with Ford when everybody was urging me to take on other makes. Remember, no company can have the best products year after year. I remained committed to Ford; and as a result, I was able to help the company change its products for the better.

I've remained basically a single-dealership business, a one- or two-store operation, because commitment matters, and this is the form of commitment that I'm comfortable with.

PART I

Business Fundamentals: What Kind of Business Do You Want to Run?

1

No Bad Dogs: Making a Lot of Money in Any Business

Making a Lot of Money in Any Business

I happen to have made a lot in the retail automobile business, but I could have done it doing just about anything. The reason is simple: The basic business principles I use will work anywhere. In any business, you need to satisfy the customer, and that's what we do at Tasca Lincoln-Mercury. Every year, we do two things: *sell a lot of product* and *make a lot of people happy*. By any meaningful measure, year after year, we're the most successful Lincoln-Mercury dealership in the world; we achieve top customer satisfaction ratings, and we're consistently among the top ten in sales volume. We do that even though we're situated poorly—in an out-of-the-way small village.

Besides being tops in customer satisfaction and among the largest in sales, we're also the most efficient. In fact, we're so efficient that we could sell new cars at cost and still make a lot of money.

How? Well, nearly every new car we sell brings us a superb, low-mileage, family-owned used car; and we make more money on them than on the new cars. I call them "useful cars," and we actually "make" those useful cars by the way we sell new cars to our customers. Nevertheless, we don't sell new cars at cost; we aim to make a fair profit by satisfying our customers, and we earn a fair profit *on every sale*. Many new-car dealers in today's market actually *lose* money on new-car sales, and that's too bad. Most of our fellow dealers deserve to make a fair profit. I hope this book helps them do that.

Who This Book Is For

This book is for *anyone in business*—whether you own the business, manage it, or work for it. I'm an automobile retailer. Does that mean that my message only applies to my fellow dealers? Not on your life. You see, while not everything we do in the car business is directly applicable to other businesses, *the way we treat people has universal application*. Every business person, not just auto dealers or other retailers, needs to understand the general principles of running a customer satisfaction–based business. If you don't, your competitors who do are going to eat you alive.

Every retailer is also a customer and wants to be treated as such. If you're not a retailer, then you're an intermediary or manufacturer in your *industry value chain*, and you have retailers like myself as your customers. How do you treat us? How should you? Remember, in life *everyone* both has customers and is a customer— somewhere in a value chain. I happen to live and work in the automobile industry value chain; you may work in a different value chain, but my customer satisfaction principles can still help you.

We all need to know how to satisfy customers—*whether our "customer" lives outside our business or inside as a co-worker*. Both *external* and *internal* customer satisfaction are important, then, and

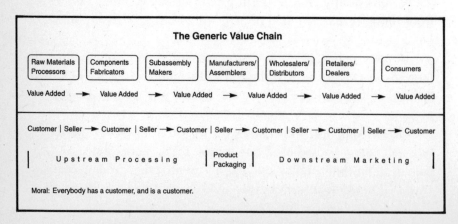

sometimes internal customer satisfaction is harder to achieve than external satisfaction. Remember, in any business, your co-worker is also your customer if the work that you personally do provides him or her with work in turn.

Increasingly today, manufacturers seek loyalty (defined as repeat purchase behavior) from their ultimate customers, the end-using consumer. More and more, their strategy is to build customer satisfaction with their branded products. Unfortunately, many manufacturers try to offset the real costs of creating customer satisfaction by squeezing their retailers. They frequently forget that their retailers are their direct customers and that their retailers often have more power to make their ultimate customers happy than they do. Remember, you don't buy an automobile from the Ford Motor Company or a competing auto maker; you buy from someone like me.

The power of retailers has, in fact, grown as product quality differences among manufacturers have shrunk so dramatically; today, there are almost no bad cars, or bad products generally. Almost everybody emphasizes high product quality to ensure they'll stay in business.

For instance, let's say that I publish books—like HarperCollins (who we as authors have as a direct, but not as an ultimate, customer). If I'm a publisher, how should I treat my bookstore "dealers"? If I squeeze bookstores on their margins and attempt to push my costs onto them *to pay for the costs to satisfy you the reader*, the bookstores in turn will be forced to squeeze you, their customer. They'll have no choice. Product selection, special customer services, and return privileges will all drop.

Now, I'm not saying that book publishers should forget about their business margins; that's a formula for disaster. What I am saying is that no manufacturer or wholesaler should pay for its ultimate customer's satisfaction out of its retailers' pockets. The ultimate customer, you the reader, will not be satisfied. As a result, everyone's business will suffer. You see, *the best way for a manufacturer to prosper is to make sure that its wholesalers and retailers make a lot of money.*

I'll tell you more about why this is true later in the book. Unfortunately, too many manufacturers seem to be jealous, rather than proud, of their retailers making money. That needs to change.

Most of the real business examples in this book are drawn from the automobile industry. As it turns out, the car business offers a multitude of particularly apt examples for illustrating the principles of customer satisfaction. Why? Well, first, we're all car buyers, and we can all understand the business and know how we like to be treated when we buy a car. Second, there is probably no business on earth where customer satisfaction matters more or is harder to deliver. If you can deliver it here, you can deliver it anywhere.

Why is satisfying prospective car buyers so tough? Because for all of us a car means _freedom;_ take away our car for even a moment, and we've lost our freedom. To satisfy a customer, we dealers have to protect your freedom—twenty-four hours a day, seven days a week. And that's a hard thing to do, because a new car is an extremely complex product and operates in some of the harshest environments possible.

A car is more complex than my personal computer, you might ask? Yes, far more so. Don't forget, the modern automobile contains _a number_ of computers, perhaps six or eight, and they're asked to operate at anything from minus 50 to more than 130 degrees Farenheit. Satisfying you, the customer, in this environment is very, very tough. Because we actually manage to do it, there's something you can learn from us.

It should also be pointed out that automobile consumers tend to be more aware than other types of consumers of brand differences and their respective customer satisfaction ratings. We all know about the J. D. Power surveys. Dave Power did both dealers and consumers a great service by creating these surveys. Having a score-card gives consumers the opportunity to make comparisons and dealers the incentive to get the job done.

Going to the Dogs!

Save money by getting rid of the firehouse mascot? The dog does not contribute much to the direct function of putting out fires. But it looks good in photographs; it makes life more pleasant for the firefighters during their boring waits for alarms; and it keeps other dogs from pissing on the equipment.

—JOHN A. SEEGER

You might say that I have two passions in life: automobiles and German shepherds. I raise and sell championship German shepherds—not to make money, but because I love the challenge. Recently, when one of my dogs won a national championship, the following headline appeared in the Ford dealerships' newspaper: "Tasca goes to the dogs!" Well, if I wanted to, I could make a lot of money in the dog business, maybe not as much as in the car business, but I could make a lot of money. And incidentally, here I'd be both a "manufacturer" and a retailer—so my principles apply to both sorts of businesses.

How would I do it? I'd apply the same business principles I use running an auto store. You may think the two businesses would be miles apart, but they're not. Making a lot of money in either case begins with my first fundamental business principle: *Sell people, not product.*

You see, selling product goes hand in hand with worrying about gross profits, continually asking the question: How much money can I make off this customer? In the dog business, that leads to schlock "volume farms" that breed poor-quality dogs for low prices. Such places abuse bitches and frequently produce puppies that carry illnesses or genetic defects. The owners of such places sell product to the pet stores so they don't have to face the final customer.

Myself, I like to deal with my customers face to face. I never sell dogs; I sell people. I like to tell customers the story of my dogs and my breeding philosophy. If I were in the dog business, part of my story would get told by my facility—neat, clean, efficient, bright, and friendly.

Dogs are a family commitment; either the customer has a family or the dog needs to become family. As a dog breeder and retailer, I'd need to know each potential buyer, know his own or his family's needs. I'd need to know the personalities. Maybe a show-quality German shepherd isn't for them or maybe a puppy isn't for them. Maybe a puppy would mean too much change in their family's routine, and they'd be better off with a more mature, house-broken dog. In that case, I'd show them another "model."

Of course, some people I'd refuse to sell to because I'd have reason to believe they'd abuse the animal.

I'd only sell quality dogs, mostly also bred by me. My commitment to breeding quality dogs would need to be complete. Expensive, you might be thinking. Well, yes—and that leads to the second principle: *Offer content, not price*. Offer what people really want in a dog. Charge the same fair price to everyone; don't try to gouge one customer to make up for the giveaway you were talked into by another customer. Offer a uniqueness based on some product or service dimension. Then you'll succeed.

Think about it, any business person can cut a price, but, using the dog-selling example again, would you as a customer want to make a long-term commitment to an animal likely to develop serious problems? Of course not. Think about the *cost* to your customer if you sell such an animal—the vet bills yes, but also the personal trauma. That's why content can beat price every time you as a business person can tell your story about what makes you special and at the same time show your customer how to obtain a lower cost in the long run.

My "dog story," then, would include my meticulous attention to breeding, my dogs' achieving competitive success, and my unique guarantee: You *will* be satisfied with your dog.

The third business principle is this: *Satisfy the customer, no matter what it takes*. Why? Remember, a satisfied customer is eight times as likely to come back to you as one who isn't satisfied, and far more likely to tell friends about you. It's that simple.

In the pet business, what might the customer come back for? Another dog perhaps, but usually that means a long trading cycle— much longer than in the new car business. *Shorten the trading cycle* is the fourth principle. I would need to offer a range of dog products and services to keep my customers coming back as well as generate new dog sales through word-of-mouth advertising from my satisfied customers.

How might I succeed in shortening the pet business trading cycle? I'd offer dog-training sessions and owner seminars. I'd also offer *expensive* dog food that would *cost* owners less. How could I do that? Well, most people feed their dogs cheap food once or twice a day. Why? They think their dogs will wolf down any amount of food given them, and that the best way to control food *costs* is to control both the *quantity* and the *price*.

That happens to be wrong. You see, a dog wolfs down its food for only one reason: It knows it's not going to get any more. Wouldn't you behave the same way if you knew there was no possibility you'd get anything to eat again for the next twelve to twenty-four hours?

Instead, free feed a dog—let it have food any time on demand—and soon it will be eating less: 17 percent less. If you go one step better and free feed a dog on *expensive* food, the dog will eat even less—because it will feel nourished without eating as much. Also, the dog will then generate less waste for you to clean up! I could sell a lot of expensive dog food, and shorten my trading cycle with my customers, by showing them how to minimize their dog food costs and their cleanup labor by free feeding on the higher-priced product. And I'd make my customers—both people and dogs—*happy* by doing it.

Let's generalize this into another customer satisfaction rule: *Always sell on customer cost; never sell on price.* Or to phrase it a bit differently, low *cost* over the usage period can beat low initial *price* every time. And, because the expensive product makes you, the retailer, more money, you can thrive by making people happy.

Let's take this point a bit further. Say you're a small retailer. How can you beat the discount chains? Find something unique to offer. If possible, base your uniqueness in something that involves your relationship to your customers. Tell the story about your business and communicate low lifetime cost, rather than trying to compete on low price. Remember, low price lasts about as long as it takes the customer to walk out your door. Above all else, *satisfy the customer.* That way, you can beat low price nearly every time. *And* you'll create customers for life.

What you might call "customer psychology" enters into satisfying the customer. You see, in any business, there are two kinds of problems: *product problems* and *people problems.* Never confuse the two. Most problems with dogs, for instance, are really people problems. If a dog is properly bred, and mine are, there are no bad dogs; there *are* people who have trouble understanding their dogs.

The way I would live out my commitment—you *will* be satisfied with your dog—would involve two things, and it's the same in any business: I would carefully match the customer to the dog, and I would offer information on the basic rules of dog and people behavior. I'd become my customers' expert in dogs, dog products, and dog behavior. You *can* be your customers' expert in your line—whether it's shoe repair, garden implements, or whatever.

If I couldn't make a customer happy with the dog, I'd take the dog back and give the customer a refund—anything to satisfy him or her. In this extreme case, taking the dog back, I'd find the dog a good home, even if that meant *giving* the dog to a family. You see, the reason most business people don't satisfy the customer is that customer satisfaction *costs*. And the minute you start looking at the cost, you won't do it. *Never look at the cost;* just do it.

A Bad Dog?

—Bob Tasca Sr.

A lady called me recently with what she termed a "dog problem." She asked if I would help her—even though she hadn't bought the animal from me. She thought maybe the breeder had sold her a bad dog. She went on to tell me she had a dog that was very *mean* to people not in her immediate family. The dog, she said, hated other people. What could she do? I asked her just one question, "What do you do with the dog when other people come to your house?" She said she locked the dog in the basement, because her visitors were afraid of dogs.

"That's what you're doing wrong," I said. "By doing that, you're ruining the dog."

She didn't understand, so I explained it to her. You see, when you treat a dog that way, the dog concludes that people must be bad. The dog thinks, "Every time people come over, I get locked up away from them. Therefore, they must be bad." That's a guaranteed way to create a mean dog. And once you've done it, it becomes very hard to undo. Why does a dog bite? Because it's not confident that it can handle you. Or crouch down and growl? Because it's warning you it's not confident with you. Never, ever separate a dog from people. And never tie a dog up.

You see, it's the same as having children. When you decide to have kids, you can't expect everything to remain the same. Things *will* change, so if you're not prepared for the changes, don't decide to have children—or to purchase a dog. Tell me, what happens to children who are told to go to their room whenever company comes? They'll grow up having people problems too, only they're more likely to take it out on you. The night you give the big party will be the night they decide to act out their anger toward you, big time. Then, unless you're prepared to admit you were wrong, they'll come to hate you.

Dogs: Not Just an Animal But a Metaphor

Do dogs resemble customers or even businesses? You bet they do. Let's take customers first. Will a customer "bite" you? You bet. How? When she comes to you, ignore her; that's equivalent to shutting the dog in the basement. Then, she'll go to someone else who doesn't treat her that way; that's her way of clamping her teeth down on you. Or she may bite you by grinding you for price. If she's treated that way—having her needs ignored—by enough business people, she'll come to hate us all.

So how do you satisfy her? First, you have to treat her as *custom*—find out what her unique needs are; don't ignore them. Next, you have to treat her as custom consistently, to earn her trust. Only then can you satisfy her.

Let's turn it around; as a customer, how can you be sure to receive customer satisfaction? Deal with someone you know you can trust and then trust that person to recommend the best for you. For example, you always get the best deal from me when you trust me to recommend what's best for you. You've doubtless heard the old business adage "The customer is always right"? Well, many times, that's wrong. Think about it, who *should* know more about your product and how it satisfies human needs than you, the retailer, the person selling it? Your customer is often *wrong*, and if you can show her where she's wrong, you can gain her trust.

Keep in mind, she knows her *needs*; never try to tell her what she needs. But you know which products will *suit* her needs; that's where she may be wrong.

As the customer satisfaction revolution grows and spreads, I predict that business people are going to become more principled than customers. By that, I mean that more customers are going to be abusing business people than the other way around. You might say that the difference between dogs and people is that dogs are more trust*worthy*.

Very often I hear other business people talk about their businesses, or certain product lines, as dogs. A typical comment runs, "If I could only get rid of that dog." There's even a way that big corporations develop their business strategies that classifies some business units or product lines as dogs.* According to this strategy, you should get rid of your dogs.

This is wrong; after all, a dog can be man's best friend. If you regard your business as a dog in the pejorative sense, it will become one. And no business is a dog if it consistently and loyally returns a fair profit to you—even if it's not huge and growing. Chances are the problem lies within you rather than within the business. Find out where you're going wrong, and then fix the problem.

Fast on the heels of the "my business is a dog" comment can usually be found, "my employees are my enemies." The surest way to make your workers your enemies is to regard them as such. At Tasca Lincoln-Mercury, we don't have employees; we only have *co-workers*—a term that may sound clichéd and euphemistic but is taken very seriously by us, I assure you. The people who work at Tasca are not adversaries; they're part of the family. The reason this relationship is so important is simple: You can't satisfy your customers until you first satisfy your workers. When your workers satisfy your customers, *then* your customers will take care of you. And you'll make a lot of money.

Yes, *even* in the dog business. Remember, there are no bad dogs; but there *are* dog owners with problems. How loyal are you to your dog? That's how loyal your dog will be to you.

Making Money in Any Business: Review of Principles

- **Sell people, not products.** Find out what your customer needs and deliver it. Don't worry about how much money you can make on the sale. The bottom line will take care of itself.

---

*See the Boston Consulting Group (BCG) Growth Matrix in a management or marketing textbook.

- **Offer content and low cost, not price.** Content will beat price any day. In all your relations with your customer, remember what it's *costing* her.

- **Satisfy the customer.** No matter what, make the customer feel satisfied. If possible, make her feel *happy.* Remember, there are two kinds of problems: product problems and people problems. Never confuse the two. Remember, too, if your customer says she has a problem, she has a problem. Never tell her, "That's normal." Don't patronize her.

- **Shorten the trading cycle.** The more often people trade with you, the more money you'll make. Find ways to make your customer want to come back to you, often. That way, you'll sell a lot of product over the long run.

If Your Business Secrets Are So Powerful, Why Do You Give Them Away?

I'm suspicious of books that purport to give the reader "proven secrets" to business success. You may wish to challenge this book on the same basis: If I'm so good, why am I revealing my principles to you—or, especially, to my competition? For that matter, if my business principles have been proven, how can they be "secrets"? If unproven, how can they be claimed to be success formulas?

Well, first of all, I believe I've shown you that my principles work to produce real business success. I've also told you that my basic business formula is no secret to Ford and Lincoln-Mercury dealers; I ran my first Ford Motor Company dealership training seminar in 1957, and I've been doing seminars ever since. Furthermore, other automobile dealers—or other business people generally—who took the trouble to figure out what I've been doing could do so fairly easily.

So why don't they? Well, *knowing* my business principles is in a sense the easier part of the problem; practicing what I preach is the tougher part.

I am giving my competition my secrets for three reasons: First, having strong competitors benefits the customer. If I really believe in customer satisfaction, and I do, then I need to do all that I can to satisfy customers—*even those who aren't mine, specifically.* Second, strong competition benefits me by forcing me to continually improve what I'm doing to stay ahead, which benefits my customers. Third, when my competitors adopt my business principles they actually make my life easier, because then we're all competing on the same customer satisfaction playing ground. I no longer have to struggle to overcome a few dealers' horse-trading practices—which, intentional or not, often result in the customer being gouged. If we all play by my rules, and I invented the rules, who do you think will come out ahead?

It's sort of like those great Vince Lombardi Green Bay Packers teams. They'd tell players on opposing teams, "Next time, we're going to run over *you*." And they would. It got to be pretty disheartening being on an opposing defense. Similarly, our competitors know what we're going to do, but the Juggernaut in Seekonk just steamrollers them anyhow. Once you've gotten the business agenda right, then it's all execution.

What can you do with the business principles I'm giving you? First, you can change your definition of where success comes from. Consistent success doesn't come from "out there" or from "getting lucky." It comes from within you. In order for you to succeed in any business, you have to get your business beliefs and your attitudes right; then you need to place bets on your own future and change the odds in your favor—and I'll tell you more about that as you read on. You need to learn to measure success in terms of achievement, not money. The money will follow, not the other way around. Next, you may need to change the way you treat your employees, or co-workers as we call them. Remember, if you take good care of your co-workers, they'll take good care of your customers. Then and only then will your customers take good care of you.

Always remember the three fundamental principles for business success: Satisfy the customer, satisfy the customer, and satisfy the customer.

Key Beliefs for Business Success

- **Customer satisfaction has universal application.** No matter what business or industry you're in, how you treat the customer is still of primary importance: Treat her fairly; always satisfy her—no matter what it takes; and if you're not sure how to treat her, treat her like you would your mother.

- **No matter what you do, commit to it wholeheartedly.** Commitment works like nothing else in life to change the odds in your favor; if you can't make the commitment, don't get involved.
- **A dog can be man's best friend.** If you regard your business or your job as a "dog" in the pejorative sense, it will become one; the problem probably lies within you rather than in the business you work for or own.
- **Never put a dollar sign on satisfying a customer; just do it.** If you look at the cost, you won't do it; and you'll lose in the long run.
- **Don't talk price; focus on cost.** Rather than cut your price, show your customer how much less it can *cost* him to do business with you over time.
- **Separate yourself from the rest.** Find some way to be unique to your customers; the most effective ways to be unique reside in how you *treat* your customers.
- **Success comes from within.** If you aren't successful, don't blame your customers or your workers or the business; instead, ask yourself, "What have *I* done wrong?"
- **Measure success in achievement, not in money.** If you measure your success in dollars, two things will happen: You won't be satisfied, and you'll be tempted to gouge your next customer to make up for the lack; money follows real achievement, not the other way around.
- **Your fellow workers are not the enemy.** Before you can satisfy your customers, you must satisfy your co-workers; then your workers will satisfy your customers, and your customers will take care of you.
- **You can't buy back a customer.** If you mistreat a customer, you can't buy her back with an attractive price; you have to *earn* her back—and that's a lot harder than if you hadn't mistreated her in the first place.

2

Betting on the Come:
Making Success Happen

Making It Happen

Most business people sit back and wait for something to happen. If they see a trend developing in the market, they may respond to it. Once a product looks like a winner, they may order it. The problem with this sort of action is simple: By the time you've taken it, it's probably too late. You've become just another holder of last season's merchandise. Manufacturers often commit the same sin: They design and package product for last season's market, then they sit back and hope something will happen. *You'll never become successful by waiting for something to happen.*

The alternative is *making it happen*. Making it happen begins with foresight—seeing opportunity in the marketplace. Remember, the marketplace is always changing. You need to judge intelligently where your market is going; then you need to find a way to capitalize on the chances you see. The critical questions are, "What will my customers want in the immediate future?" and "What will satisfy them?"

There are ways to identify today the directions that a market will take tomorrow. I'll talk to you about that later in Chapter 11, "Even the Undertakers Wouldn't Buy." The point I want to make here is this: Spotting opportunity doesn't have to be difficult or all that risky—*if* you learn to read the signposts that point toward your market's future direction.

Finding opportunity in your market doesn't have to involve anything terribly complex; it all comes down to knowing your customers and their needs. For instance, in our business we recently did quite well by ordering in all of our mid-priced product with dual airbags and antilock brakes, when our competitors were still ordering in cheaper product without them. We bet that customers now wanted these safety features and would pay the extra money to get them. As it turned out, we were right. Having an idea about where your market is going, however, is not enough.

Betting on the Come

You may depend upon it, sir, the knowledge that he shall be hanged in a fortnight concentrates a man's mind wonderfully.

—SAMUEL JOHNSON

If you don't order in a lot of inventory or make a lot as a manufacturer, you'll never flourish. If you don't make a commitment to selling a lot of product, you'll never see a big reward. The simple truth is this: Satisfying your customers will never give you a sense of achievement or make you a lot of money *if you don't have many customers*. And "many customers" presupposes a prior inventory commitment. You can follow all the principles so far discussed in this book and never succeed if you fail to place inventory and other bets on your future. In fact, *there are only two ways to run a business: betting on the come and betting on the came.*

What do I mean?

Betting on the *came* means sitting back and waiting for something to happen; chances are, it'll never happen. Betting on the *come* means making it happen *by placing a bet on an outcome, a bet on what you believe you can make happen in the future.* Take some *irreversible* action today, such as ordering in a lot of new product, that you'll have to follow through on tomorrow with actions designed to make your *customers happy and your business grow.*

It's the same thing for a manufacturer; every time a manufacturer introduces a new product, the company, unknowingly or not, places a big bet on the come—on management's ability to sell a lot of units. Successful betting on the come may be even more important for manufacturers than for wholesalers and retailers. When a car maker, for instance, introduces a major new model, the investment to be recouped is so great that, in effect, management is betting the company on its ability to sell a lot of new product.

Six Hundred Strippers:
A Story about Betting on the Come

—John Pagano, a Tasca co-worker

Back in 1963, Bob [Sr.] got a call from Ford Regional Sales. "Bob, we have a six-hundred-car fleet order that the buyer just canceled. How many can we put you down for?"

The fleet cars, of course, were what we call strippers; they had the least amount of feature content possible. No retail customer would buy one unless he couldn't afford anything else. Corporate fleet accounts ordered them because their employees had to drive them. Bob told the Ford Regional guy, "You poll the other [New England Ford] dealers; and what they won't take, I will."

Regional called back about a week later. "How many do you have left?" Bob asked.

"Six hundred," came the reply.

"All right, I'll take them."

Now even though Tasca Ford was selling about seven thousand cars a year at that time, six hundred cars that were a mistake and wouldn't sell retail represented a big gamble. How were we going to sell another six hundred units beyond what we already had on the lot? Bob knew they wouldn't sell as they were; he also knew that many of his customers craved something a little different, something unique. So, he set about doing what he calls "waking up the car." He found within Ford Motor's parts inventories bits and pieces that would make the six hundred strippers look different—such as an anodized aluminum side trim piece from an Econoline van. Those were the days when Americans accepted, and even loved, lots of chrome accent pieces. When Bob got done, the former strippers looked like a totally new car line from Ford. Bob promoted them as "the T–63, available only at Tasca Ford." They sold like hotcakes.

In fact, they did so well that some of the other New England Ford dealers through the dealer association charged Ford with dealer favoritism—providing a special product to Tasca only. A lawyer from Ford came down, and Bob showed him where every special part came from—right out of the Ford parts catalogs. Bob had guessed that some dealers would respond that way; that's why he told the Ford regional guy to poll the other dealers first to find out how many they'd take.

Some people, out of jealousy maybe, would call what Bob did a sales gimmick; I'd call it betting on the come. Bob bet more than eight hundred thousand dollars up front that he could wake up those strippers and sell them. And he did. Incidentally, they were very profitable for the dealership.

MORAL:

When the product's manufacturer doesn't make it happen, you need to.

In the computer business, chip makers and software houses sometimes make bets of similar magnitude. In such situations, one bad bet can nearly sink you. The Chrysler Airflow was an example of such a bet that failed, as were the RCA and GE bets on the computer market. Taurus and the 360, on the other hand, were Ford and IBM bets that triumphed in the marketplace. Retailers and wholesalers rarely have so much riding on a bet.

Thus betting on the come first of all means commitment. It means making a commitment with myself today for what I believe I can do tomorrow. Then it means keeping that commitment, making my commitment happen. Last, it means translating my personal commitment into similar commitments toward making it happen on the part of my co-workers.

After all, if I don't make positive commitments to my business's future, how can I expect my workers to do so? On the other hand, if my co-workers don't place their own bets on their futures, how can I succeed in making my bet happen?

Betting on the come means taking risks. That scares many people. But in business, the riskiest thing you can do is to try nothing.

Then the market changes, and you don't. What bet on your future would *you* be willing to make now?

A Blank Check

—John Pagano, a Tasca co-worker

Bob Tasca over the years has tried all sorts of ways to give his salesmen incentives to improve their performances. Complacency is the enemy. Once during the mid-1960s the Tasca Ford dealership was experiencing one of those periods of complacency. Bob knew it from the poor close ratios the salesmen had. We had plenty of [showroom] traffic but poor sales. He also knew it was up to him to change the situation, that he needed to lead his men out of it. At the time, Tasca Ford employed twenty salesmen.

Bob walked into his sales meeting the beginning of one week, and he announced that he had twenty blank checks in his hand. He passed them out, one to each man. You need to understand, these were *live* checks, signed by Bob Tasca himself—with no money amount entered. He said to them, "I want you to fill out your own paychecks for next week. What do you think you could sell if you really applied yourself?"

At first, the men just grinned at one another. It was like a dream come true—being given a real blank check. Just fill it out for any amount you wanted! Then reality began to set in; the grins disappeared. The men began to realize that whatever amount they put down they'd be on the line for, that you'd have to back up whatever you put down on that piece of paper. It ceased to be a game; it became very serious business. And it worked. The proof was in the sales jump that week. What Bob was asking them to do personally was to bet on the come.

MORAL:

You need to challenge your people to place their own bets on the future.

The Worst Mistake You Can Make

When you've dug yourself into a hole in the ground, don't keep digging.

—Margaret Thatcher

Like it or not, business is inherently risky; all sorts of things, many of them bad, might happen to you. All sorts of things could go wrong; and the more you think about them, *the more likely they are to happen*. If you sit back and think about how your business could go downhill, it will. Why? You'll have shut yourself off to the big gains on opportunities that could make your business go uphill.

You see, business is always changing; the markets for the products I sell continually evolve. Chances are the way I made money last year will not be the way I make it this year. If you don't like this reality, then maybe you need to be doing something else. Ask yourself what *you're* doing wrong that keeps your business from selling a lot and satisfying your customers. Then ask yourself if you're willing to change *yourself* to fix the business. If you're not, then you need to get out. If you *are*, then you need to start betting on the come. The worst mistake in business is to do nothing.

Letting My People Down

A conversation that took place between Bob Tasca Sr. and Peter Caldwell in the spring of 1992:

Bob: I don't know what I'm doing wrong. Last month, I spent forty-five thousand dollars on advertising in the *Providence Journal,* and I haven't come anywhere near getting it back in car sales. I'm doing something wrong.

Peter: Hey, it's the economy. The economy's just plain lousy.

Bob: No, that's not it. I'm doing something wrong. You know, when I get up in the morning, I point a finger at the guy in the mirror, and I say, "You, you S.O.B.! You're the problem." When I figure out what it is I'm doing wrong, I'll fix it.

One month later:

Bob: I figured out what I was doing wrong. I was letting my people down. So, I went out and ordered seven hundred more new cars, and in my sales meetings, I told my salesmen to go out and sell them. You know what? It's working!

MORALS:

1. Never let your co-workers think you're afraid of the future.
2. If you're going to blame someone for not making it happen, blame yourself.

Doing nothing is the riskiest course of action, because the market is almost certainly going to change. When it does, almost any other action will have better odds of success than this approach: "I'll keep doing what I've been doing in the past." At such times, doing nothing different is like digging yourself into a hole in the ground—and continuing to dig. When you've dug yourself into a hole, *stop digging!*

And that doesn't mean do nothing; it means *change* what you're doing. Of course, it's best to change *before* you've dug a hole in the ground. That means placing a new bet on the come *before* it's obvious to your competition that the present bets will soon stop paying off.

Does all this mean that running a business is tantamount to shooting craps? Not at all. You see, in shooting dice or in any other pure game of chance, the odds are fixed. They are what they are. In business, they aren't. Properly speaking, business is not *risky* at all; rather, it's more accurate to say that it involves uncertainty. The important distinction is that in business I can *change* the odds. Making a bet on my future success means I'll be motivated to find a way to win: *My commitment itself* changes the odds in my favor.

The way that I most often change the odds to favor me is to order in a lot of inventory. Then I have to find a way to sell it. Norman Vincent Peale might call it the "power of positive thinking." I suppose there's something to that. But it also harks back to that Samuel Johnson quotation that appeared earlier in this chapter. It's true; nothing so concentrates a person's mind as a mountain of inventory to sell.

Failing Forward

Be not afraid.

—JESUS OF NAZARETH

Most business people are terrified of failure. They also tend not to be very kind to subordinates who appear to have failed them. What's the first thing most managements do when sales are down? Fire the sales manager. When they do, they violate the first principle of problem solving in business: *Never place blame; always fix what's gone wrong. Fix the problem.* There's always only one person you should blame when things go wrong—and that's you yourself as management. Find out where *you've* gone wrong and fix that first. Chances are the problem will then begin to take care of itself.

Nobody in a Tasca business has ever gotten fired for failing. Some people have gotten promoted for their failures. At Tasca there are only three things that can earn you an invitation to leave: not caring about the customer, doing something wrong and then lying about it, and failing to try. I just love people who really try— even if they're wrong, even if they fail at first. You see, there's nothing wrong with failing—provided you *fail forward.* By that, I mean learning from your mistakes. Failing forward doesn't mean learning never to try again; that's wrong. Rather, it means learning what doesn't work as part of finding what does work. Failing forward means taking the information from one failed bet on the come and using it to reduce your chances of failing on your next bet. In a sense, then, failure isn't failure at all—it's information. At least, it *can* be, provided the person is paying attention.

In our businesses, we regularly make bets that we know will fail—all as a part of an experimentation process that helps us know on what to bet heavily. For instance, every season I order in one car of each color; I know some of those colors will be failed bets—my customers won't like them. I also have a pretty good idea which ones will fail—but I want to know for sure. Then, I do two things: I unload the failed bets quickly, and I order in a lot of product in the five fastest-selling colors.

Complacency Is the Enemy

Too many of us in business think that co-workers who're willing to take a chance and place a bet on the come are our enemies. That's just as wrong as the commonly held attitudes toward failure. The real enemy is complacency. As an employer, you should *cherish* co-workers who care enough about your future and their own to take a chance—to bet on the come.

In fact, one of the hardest things in business is *overcoming* complacency and encouraging your co-workers to place their own personal bets on the come. Too many employees think that just because they get a paycheck each week everything's fine at work, and they don't need to try harder. The problem is that they've never had to sign the *front* of a check; they've only signed on the *back*. Placing a bet on the come makes your co-worker an entrepreneur. Don't punish her. Reward her.

Betting on the Come: Review of Principles

- **You've only got two choices.** In business, you either make it happen or you let it happen to you; either you're *betting on the come* or *betting on the came.*
- **Bet on the come.** This means placing a bet today on some outcome that you believe you can accomplish in the future. Take some *irreversible* action today, such as ordering in a lot of new inventory, that forces you to follow through and make something happen in your business tomorrow. In doing so, *strive to make your customers happy.*
- **Remember, nothing can be worse than nothing.** The worst thing you can do in business is nothing; when you do nothing, you're almost certain to be wrong.
- **Betting on the come is the safest course.** It reduces your chance of failure, because you commit yourself to making the desired outcome happen.
- **Fail forward.** Use failure as information to better chart your future steps; don't be afraid.
- **Remember, your co-workers will do as they see you do.** If you won't make a commitment to the future, why expect them to?

3

Sell a Lot of Product: Make a Lot of People Happy

An Early Lesson in Life

I learned very early that if I satisfied a customer with repairs, she tended to come back the next time her car needed service. I also learned that if an unhappy customer ever came back, it was to complain.

—Bob Tasca Sr.

started in the automobile business on May 5, 1943, as a forty-cent-an-hour grease monkey. I was sixteen years old then, and I'd been fixing cars ever since I was four, when I first worked on a Model A Ford. My father told me I was crazy going into the automobile business, that there was no future in it, and that I could make more money—over a dollar an hour—working in the jewelry business. (The jewelry business was the manufacturing mainstay in Rhode Island then.)

I went ahead anyway, because ever since eighth grade I'd known what I wanted to be. That year in school, our teacher asked us to write a career book on what we wanted to do in life. I wrote that I wanted to be a Ford dealer. That's never changed. Only once was I tempted to go a different route, and that had to do with my love of music: I wanted to be a part of the Glenn Miller Band. In fact, I once had the opportunity to solo for them.

The opportunity arose when I was working backstage where the band was performing. When the regular sax player became ill, I got the nod. But by then, Miller was dead, and I'd returned to my first love, Ford automobiles.

Working as a mechanic, I learned very early that if you satisfied a customer—fixed her car right the first time, got it ready on time, made sure you didn't leave any grease on the steering wheel—she would most likely come back to you. If you *didn't* fix it right the first time, you had an unhappy customer. She might come back; but if she did, it was to complain.

Satisfying the customer became paramount for me. Over a period of seven years with a local Ford dealer, I went from grease monkey to apprentice mechanic to used-car mechanic to used-car buyer to used-car manager, and then to sales manager and general manager. And in each position, I aimed to satisfy my customers.

Working at these various jobs, it became increasingly apparent that the *secret to success in any business is latching on to a customer and never losing him*. If you repair his car, you want to keep repairing his car forever. If you sell her a car, you want to sell her every time she needs another one. You don't ever want the customer to go anywhere else. Today at Tasca Lincoln-Mercury we have a saying about our customers: "Until *debt* do us part." That is, as long as you can afford an automobile, we want to be your automobile dealer.

By 1950, I was pretty successful by most people's measures: I was general manager of a good-sized Ford dealership. Two momentous things happened in my life that year: I got married, and I quit my job—all at the same time. In fact, I wrote my resignation letter on my honeymoon. That was a little scary for my wife, knowing that we wouldn't have an income when we got back home. Why did I quit? The person I was working for knew about customer satisfaction, but he didn't *practice* it. When it got to the point at which I wasn't able to satisfy the customers as I wanted to due to company policy, I left.

I left a very well-paying position, incidentally. And I left a man who'd come to regard me almost as if I were a son. But there is nothing more important than acting with integrity.

As I've already told you, I've been married to the same woman now for over forty-five years and I've been a Ford Motor Company dealer for almost the same period of time. I've felt from day one that nothing is more important than satisfying customers. *I can't sleep nights* when my customers are unhappy; I mean that. So, when I couldn't satisfy my customers where I worked, there was no reason for me to remain in the business—*because I knew it would eventually fail.*

When I got back from my honeymoon, I started my own used-car dealership. Then, after a long struggle, I was able to get a franchise to sell Ford products in Bristol, Rhode Island. At age twenty-seven, I became a Ford dealer—on November 17, 1953, to be exact. I was the youngest Ford dealer in the country. It was a small account; I started off with 1.5 employees (one of them was me) in a rented eight-by-ten office in Dupont's Service Station. I got the dealership because nobody else wanted it, and I began with two thousand dollars in cash—which was more than thirty thousand dollars less than the normal minimum Ford required.

In those days, most Ford dealers were small, community-based operations. I was supposed to sell thirty-five cars a year, which is about three a month. The first month I was open, I sold twenty-six. That was almost the entire first year's quota. Within two months, I had the thirty-five thousand dollars I was supposed to be capitalized at in the bank. Within six months, we'd moved to a permanent facility right on the water of Narragansett Bay. It was a lovely spot—until hurricane Carol swept it all away on August 31, 1954.

I started all over again on high ground, this time temporarily at 57 Taunton Avenue in East Providence. The permament facility, where I unknowingly met Ernie Breech, opened at 777 Taunton Avenue on December 20, 1956, and soon became known as "777" to our customers, the Ford Motor Company, and other Ford dealers worldwide. It became *very* well known, in fact, for by 1960, 777 was selling more than seven thousand new and used cars and trucks annually.

You may well wonder how we managed to go from nothing to second largest in the world in just seven years. Clearly, it was something beyond people liking me and wanting to buy a car from me. I *do* like people, and people tend to like me—but that doesn't mean they'll necessarily do business with me. It had to be something *beyond* that, beyond the personal charisma of a salesman.

What the *beyond* thing involved was giving the customer superlative service—service such as he'd never had or even imagined. Offering evening and weekend service, quick service, and pick-up and delivery; getting up in the middle of the night to make a lost key; retrieving a car that had broken down and giving the customer a car to drive home in—I did all of these things very early in life, because I thought it would distinguish my business from the competition.

I can remember getting out of bed in the middle of the night and driving down to Fall River—nearly twenty miles away—to pick up a customer's car that had broken down. The customer phoned, saying, "I broke down on the highway and left the car right there. I was able to get a ride to Providence, and I got home with a cab, but my car is right in the middle of the road, and I wish you'd have it picked up."

What was I supposed to tell him? "Call us in the morning, and we'll take care of it"? He was concerned about the car being left the way it was, afraid that it might be towed and that he'd get charged with leaving the car improperly parked. So I went down and handled it. And you know what? That man bought cars from me for the rest of his life. I probably sold him eight or ten cars because of that incident.

You could say that at Tasca Ford we *invented* customer satisfaction before people had even come up with the name for it.

How Most People Do Business: The Gross Profit Business Agenda

Caveat emptor [Let the buyer beware].

In the long run, we'll all be dead.

—JOHN MAYNARD KEYNES

Most business people—not just some *car dealers*, I'm convinced—begin their projections of what they can hope to do in a business by focusing on a product, and they ask, "How much can I sell that product for?" That type of thinking leads to what I call a "gross profit business agenda." If there's a range of products under consideration, they ask, "Which one carries the highest profit margin?"

For example, many customers prefer Michelin tires. That's why the automobile companies have been putting them on certain new cars now for decades. I'm not saying they're necessarily better than other tire brands, just that some customers *perceive* them to be better. Most replacement tire companies, though, hate to sell Michelins. Do you know why? Because the companies make a smaller margin on them than on some of the other brands. You don't have to be a genius, then, to guess which brand they don't encourage the customer to buy.

The next thing most business people focus on is getting the maximum effective price the market will bear *in each transaction.* I happen to come from an industry where this practice is common. In the retail automobile business, every transaction is likely to have a different set of numbers. Every customer is literally treated *differently*, depending on his or her respective bargaining powers. But car dealers are not unique. In other industry value chains, businesses achieve the same result by a variety of techniques, such as bait-and-switch tactics and carrying a multitude of quality levels for the same basic product.

You see, Americans have come to believe that the higher the price is, the higher the quality will be. That may or may not be true, but clearly the typical business segments its overall market by selling essentially the same product at several different prices. The higher-priced versions yield the business a greater absolute profit per transaction, and sometimes a greater relative profit as well. Most businesses don't engage in these margin-boosting practices one on one, eyeball to eyeball, with the customer as those in the auto industry do, but they engage in them nevertheless via company policy.

Curiously, business people who follow the gross profit business agenda also emphasize competing on price. They use a low price to get the customer in the door, and then get him to switch to a higher-priced model or jack up the price at delivery time.

That's what the so-called low-ball was all about in the auto business years ago. You'd settle on a price so low that it might even be below your cost—anything to get the customer to buy; then, at delivery time you'd find a reason to jack up the price and tell the customer to take it or leave it. Well, often the customer wanted that new car so badly he could taste it, and he'd pay.

Fortunately, those sorts of practices aren't legal anymore. But the point is, these methods are all designed to compete on price, which implies willingness to cut a price. And yet, they're practiced by business people who're seeking to maximize gross profit based on price. There's a contradiction in that.

The third thing most business people focus on is their cost of doing business with the customer, which along with price and merchandise cost determines gross profit. A variety of techniques are used to keep the firm's *cost of sales* down. Service charges, restocking fees, and limits on merchandise returns are some of the obvious ones directly affecting the customer.

Supermarkets, particularly, have a reputation for lowering sales costs by taking advantage of higher margins offered by competing suppliers. Yet, most of the savings from those deals never get passed on to the customer; instead, they go to gross profit. Now, my point isn't to condemn supermarkets; they operate on some of the tightest margins in the world. The thing that concerns me is the *hidden cost* that is incurred by not satisfying the customer. Sure, it costs money, often a lot of it, to make customers happy. But it's usually worth it. If you focus on the dollars you're using to satisfy the customer, you'll never spend them.

It has always seemed strange to me that the same business people who'll spend large sums on a physical plant won't spend anything more than the acceptable minimum on customer satisfaction. I guess having a big, impressive building is an ego thing. Or maybe big buildings communicate security to some customers.

Myself, I like small, very efficient stores—because I hate to spend money on overhead. If I can keep my facility small and running efficiently, I can spend the overhead savings on customer satisfaction and still make as much money as my competitor with her knock-'em-dead emporium. In fact, over the long run, I'll make a lot more than she will, because I'll have the repeat business. For my competitor, there might not *be* a long run.

Let me tell you a little bit about how the gross profit business agenda gets played out in my industry and show you why it's so self-defeating. I'm choosing to talk about the automobile business here, both because I know it best and because it's a business with which everyone is familiar.

The retail auto store is one of the few left where business is still sometimes transacted like in a Middle Eastern bazaar—call it horse-trading or camel trading or whatever. The customer walks into a typical auto dealership, and what does she encounter? A salesman who gets paid a commission based on the gross profit he's able to make off her. The level of his earnings that week in part depends on how much he can get her to pay. She might not know that, but *he* sure does.

Nor is the ensuing bargaining going to happen on a level playing field. Chances are he knows both the cost of his product and the value of her trade-in; and chances are she doesn't know either one. Not only that, it may well be that the previous few customers the salesman dealt with were sharp bargainers, and he got beat down. So, he's going to be out to make as much as he can off her.

Chances are, too, that she's going to want more car, more of what I call "creature features," than she can afford. So what does the salesman do—*after* she's agreed to the highest price he can bargain out of her? He turns her over to the dealership's Finance and Insurance (F&I) Department personnel who're supposed to "help" her afford the heavily optioned car she may have just agreed to pay too much for. The F&I Department proceeds to bury her in debt. Which is why I call a traditional F&I department the *burial squad*.

You see, these days most customers have gotten pretty good at bargaining for price; so good, in fact, that many car dealerships actually *lose* money on new car sales. These dealerships must then rely on the F&I Department to make back the profit they lost on the car's selling price.

How does the F&I Department do it? Two ways. First, it encourages the customer to take on a long-term mortgage—typically a four- or five-year auto loan. If she does, the dealership makes money on the spread between the wholesale and retail money rates on that loan. The customer usually doesn't know that—doesn't realize that the dealership is making money by putting her into such a loan. All she notices is that the monthly payment offered by the dealership seems to be lower than if she were to go directly through a bank; so she takes the deal.

The other way the F&I Department may help recapture the dealership's profit is through selling the customer insurance and other products that are either overpriced or that she doesn't really need. A classic example is undercoating. Undercoating is not only something new cars don't need, it may actually be *harmful*—if it clogs drainage holes in the underbody. But undercoating makes the dealership a bundle; F&I can charge the customer two hundred dollars for a product that costs the dealership maybe fifty dollars. F&I also makes the dealership money on extended service contracts, putting Scotchgard on the upholstery (another needless product today; auto upholstery material comes with Scotchgard), and various insurance policies.

After F&I gets done with her, where's the customer? What is the *cost* to her of that *low* monthly payment? She's now driving "upside down" as we say in the trade; for much of the period of the loan, her car will be worth less—at first much less—in the marketplace than the outstanding principle on the loan. Getting out of the deal will cost her a bundle. And it's likely that, after she's paid off the loan, she'll feel pressured to keep the car a while to forestall as long as possible going through another such experience.

Now, let's consider what's happened to each player in this ritualized sport of auto horse trading.

What the dealer has accomplished falls into two categories. First, he's achieved the gross profit objective: The dealership has made the maximum single-transaction gross profit off the customer on the *front end*. That is, he's captured in one lump sum *at the time of sale* nearly all his likely gains from trade with that customer *over her lifetime*. Why? Because of the second accomplishment: The dealer, by burying the customer in debt and putting her upside down, has effectively taken her out of the new car market for six to seven years.

Think about it. How likely is it that this customer will go back to that same dealer again, some seven years later? With performance such as this, is it really surprising that the traditional automobile dealership has a customer loyalty rating of well under 20 percent—that fewer than one in five buyers become repeat-purchase customers? Or that the average trading cycle in the new car business has been about six years?

I call this a lose-lose game. The dealer lost the chance to have a customer for life; the customer lost the opportunity to enjoy a new car every few years for possibly less money than it cost her to drive the same one for seven years. It all happened not because the dealership owner personally wished to mistreat her, but because of this simple truth: *The gross profit business agenda always leads to both players losing over the long run.*

Notice that this outcome will be true for any gross profit agenda business in any industry—not just the auto business: The same principles hold, and they produce the same outcomes.

Gross Profit Business Agenda Principles

- **Maximize gross profit per transaction.** Charge what each market, even what each customer, will bear.
- **Minimize after-sale costs.** Avoid paying out money for customer satisfaction.
- **Make profits on the front end.** Don't worry about customers over the long run; maybe they, or you, won't be around then anyhow.

I believe that most auto dealers—and most business people generally—would like to treat their customers fairly; they'd *love* to have satisfied customers. Then why don't they?

Because they don't know *how* to. Many business people are caught in a trap—the "Gross Profit Trap"—and they don't see a way out. They compete on price to try to make money, and they get beaten down to nothing. Please understand me, I'm not being critical of my fellow dealers here. I'm telling you the way it is, in many different businesses today.

Most of my fellow dealers today don't make too much money selling cars—they make too little! Some of them are practically *giving away* the fair profit they should realize on each sale. I'd like to help them change that. That's part of the reason I'm writing this book. Does that mean that their customers will get hurt when the dealers start earning fair profits? By no means. Unless a dealer-ship—or any other business—makes a fair profit, it can't possibly satisfy its customers.

Too many businesses today have run into the paradox of the gross profit business agenda: When you try to make money by max-imizing your gross profit, you end up losing money. If *you're* some-one who's caught in this trap and living out the paradox, there *is* a better way. Read on.

The Customer Satisfaction Business Agenda

The secret is to make profits one slice at a time, not go for the whole loaf. Low price goes away as soon as the customer walks out your door; satisfaction lasts, often a lifetime.

—BOB TASCA SR.

At the Tasca family dealerships, we do things differently. You could say that we don't follow the same rules. To begin with, at Tasca *you can't pay too much for a car.* Now that's an amazing thing to say, but it's true. You can't pay too much for a car, because we won't let you. Every new car we sell gets menu-priced. What that means is that if we have one hundred identically equipped GS Mercury Sables on the lot, every one of those cars will get sold at *exactly the same price*. That price allows us to make a fair profit on the front end in exchange for selling you the car and preparing it for delivery.

Incidentally, I'm a stickler for product preparation; it must be absolutely right or it doesn't go out of here. That means we don't have to try to make up for a low selling price by burying the cus-tomer in F&I. Our F&I Department is purely a customer service department. We make very little money on financing, and nothing gets sold except authorized Ford Motor Company service contracts, Ford-approved alarm systems, and state-approved life insurance policies. F&I is there only to inform and help the customer.

Don't get caught in a thinking trap here. Menu pricing isn't only an auto dealer's concept. Applied in a generalized way, what I'm advocating here is *consistent* pricing at a *fair* profit for *any* busi-ness. For a business person, it means not having to compete on price (translation: not burying yourself through discounting you can't afford); for customers it means knowing you didn't have to pay more than the next person and that you'll be satisfied in your dealings. Does *your* business advertise "lowest prices in town"? Wouldn't you like to be free of that?

We also don't get caught up in the internal contradictions of the gross profit business agenda. We don't compete on price; there's just one price, and we don't come down on price to beat another dealer. Because we don't compete on price, we don't try to maximize profits on each deal either. We don't have to, because we don't do losing deals that we then have to try to make up for. We aim to make the same fair profit on each deal—I call it making profits one slice at a time. We don't try to get the whole customer lifetime profit loaf all at once.

What happens is that we make a fair profit on the front end and a fair profit on the back end on service; and, we expect to earn the customer's repeat new car business. Last, we don't consider the cost of satisfying the customer. My co-workers each have a *blank check* to satisfy the customer—whatever it takes. And that's costly. But we make up for the cost by running the most efficient auto dealership in the world.

If we don't compete on price, then how do we compete? Three ways. We compete on product content, on customer satisfaction, and on *cost* to the customer. You see, most people would rather have a nicely equipped automobile than a stripper. But they feel they have to buy less car to make it affordable. What they tend not to realize is that the stripped car is worth less at trade-in than the nicely equipped car—significantly less. It turns out, we can show the customer a way to have the car with creature features—and have it *cost* him no more than the stripped car he didn't want in the first place. So, we order in only cars that have the most desirable features and will have the best resale value for the customer. That is, we offer content and low *cost to drive*, not low price.

Then, we make the commitment to the customer that he absolutely *will* be satisfied with our product and with our sales and our service teams. If not, we'll give him his money back. Besides financial cost, we'll save the customer worry regarding whether he'll be satisfied with the car and the service, and we'll save him the physical cost associated with frustrating trips to the dealer. Obviously, he didn't intend to buy a car with problems. So, if problems come up, we'll fix them. If we can't fix them, we'll buy the car back. You see, that way *content can beat low price every time*.

There's only one thing you can't get at a Tasca dealership—and that's a fancy showroom or waiting room. We don't have big, new, dramatic buildings. We don't have things like chandeliers in the show-room or fancy fixtures in the rest rooms. There *was* a chandelier in the showroom at Tasca Ford when I bought it back; I moved it to where it would be less conspicuous. We're not a country club dealership. We offer unparalleled customer satisfaction—*to the common people*.

The Three-Thousand-Dollar Difference: A Story

—John Pagano, a Tasca co-worker

A customer came into the Ford store late in the day one Ash Wednesday. He wanted to buy a new truck. We were three thousand dollars higher than some other dealer, he said. He wanted to know why, and he wanted us to come down on price. Part of the reason was that we stock only trucks that are equipped for high resale value; the other dealer was offering the guy different options. Still, he wanted us to beat the other dealer's price. The salesman couldn't seem to satisfy him. It was getting to be a problem on the floor. Bob was leaving shortly to go to Mass, and he personally needed to sell another vehicle like he needed a hole in the head. But he couldn't pass up the chal-lenge: He just *had* to sell this guy, to show that he could do it. So he went out and spoke to the customer.

"Let's compare apples to apples," he said. "At the other dealer, can you get serviced on a weekend?"

"Well, no."

"Can you get emergency service and repairs at ten o'clock at night?"

"No."

"What if you blow a transmission plowing snow? Will the other dealer take care of you and have you out the same day or night?"

"No."

"Will he give you your money back if you're not satisfied with the vehicle?"

"No."

"Well then, you're not comparing apples to apples are you?"

"No, I guess not."

"And now let's talk *cost* to you, not *price*. If I show you that it will actually cost you less over two years to pretrade for more truck at Tasca than to borrow money on a four-year loan to buy less truck at the other dealer, will you do business with me? Wouldn't you rather have a new truck every two years than own one for four, if it doesn't cost you any more?"

Well, suffice it to say the guy did business with Bob, and the price was still three thousand dollars higher than the other dealer's. And Bob made it to Ash Wednesday evening Mass. This is what Bob means when he says that content and low cost can beat price every time—*if* you have a unique story to tell and you tell it to the customer, rather than just doing arithmetic.

MORAL:

Content can beat price every time if you tell your story rather than just do arithmetic.

Consider what happens when a new customer walks into a Tasca dealership. First, she's not met by a salesperson. She's met by a Tasca co-worker called a "greeter." It's the greeter's job to make the customer feel comfortable, to get information on who she is, and to assign her to the salesperson best able to relate well to her. The salesperson she then meets with has only three things to do: determine her needs, demonstrate product, and tell her the Tasca customer satisfaction story. There's no high pressure applied and there's no bargaining on price. We do everything we can to avoid an adversarial relationship. While some other dealers' salespeople are busy doing arithmetic, figuring out how they can make more money off the customer, my salesperson will be busy convincing the customer that no matter what, she *will* be satisfied at Tasca. We'll do anything, even give her money back, to make her happy.

Can you use a customer greeter in your business? Well, I know that Wal-Mart found they could. It started out as one store manager's attempt to reduce shoplifting by stationing a worker at the door. Soon, thanks to an individual worker's initiative, the job became one of helping people as they came *in*. Obviously, the worker assigned to the job loved people and preferred to help them rather than police them. Well, the idea got adopted by the whole chain. Does this give you an idea for *your* business?

After reaching an agreement with a salesperson, the customer goes to F&I where she's actually *helped*. Our F&I people are trained to provide honest information and to process her order; they don't pressure her to buy anything. The dealership makes very little money in F&I. It's purely a customer service, part of our pledge that You *Will* Be Satisfied.

So let's put it all together into the complete "Customer Satisfaction Business Agenda"—*my* business agenda. I begin with *betting on the come:* If you're going to flourish in a customer satisfaction business, you need to sell a lot of product. That means betting on the come: order in a lot, sell a lot. It doesn't mean cutting your price to the bone; that's practicing *leadership into receivership*. The reason you need to bet on the come is that you need to *make a lot of people happy* to gain the volume necessary to cover the costs of customer satisfaction. Otherwise, you'll never make a lot of money my way—in any business.

The second thing is satisfying the customer. Here's where not considering the cost comes in. In satisfying customers, we never consider the cost; we just do it. My co-workers literally have a blank check to satisfy the customer. Customer satisfaction starts when the customer first walks in and gets greeted by Gene or one of our other greeters. It ends only when the customer can't afford to do business with us anymore. We'll satisfy a customer until debt do us part.

The third element in the customer satisfaction business agenda is shortening the trading cycle. In my industry, the average new car trading cycle is about six years. At Tasca Lincoln-Mercury, our trading cycle is twenty-nine months; our customers trade on the average of every two and a half years. Our goal is to get that down to under two years. Now, if your customers trade every six years and mine trade every two years, and everything else is equal, who's going to make more money, in any business?

The Customer Satisfaction Business Agenda

- **Sell a lot of product; make a lot of people happy.** Focus on selling a lot of product, not on making a large gross profit on each product you sell.
- **Focus on customer satisfaction.** No matter what it costs, satisfy the customer; if possible, make her *happy,* so she does business with you again. Remember, a satisfied customer is *eight* times more likely to repeat his or her purchase than a dissatisfied customer.
- **Shorten the trading cycle.** Make your repeat business happen more often; if my customers trade with me every two time periods and yours trade with you every six time periods and everything else is equal, who's going to make more money?

By the way, this point about shortening the trading cycle shouldn't be construed as only applying to businesses that sell big-ticket items—such as automobiles and yachts—where trading in still-valuable used product for new product predominates. Think of the trading cycle as being how often your customer comes back to you to buy.

Seen from that perspective, trading cycle becomes relevant to *every* business. The end goal of a customer satisfaction business is customer loyalty, creating customers for life. Obviously, one way you build a lifetime relationship with anyone is by seeing him or her more often—whether it's in marriage or business. Absence doesn't make the heart grow fonder; it makes the heart forgetful. It makes your customers forget why they did business with you in the first place. The ultimate answer to forgetful hearts and failing businesses is shortening the trading cycle.

Let me give you just one example—from the major appliances industry. Major appliance retailers have a tough job keeping customers loyal, as do major appliance manufacturers, because the trading cycle is both long and of *uncertain length* and because service and repairs happen very infrequently.

Who knows when that washing machine will fail? In ten years? In twenty years? Nobody knows, but it's going to be a long time.

Given that uncertainty, how can you as a dealer or manufacturer keep your customers loyal? Well, as a dealer, you can introduce lines of minor appliances that get traded far more often. As a manufacturer, you can do the kind of reminder advertising that made the "Maytag Man" famous, although that's a very tough thing to do effectively. And it can be very costly.

As a manufacturer, you might also try to both increase product content (and price to the customer) and innovate in purchase terms—all at the same time. You might *rent* more technologically advanced products and create secondary markets for such products in used condition. That would lower the customer's cost and trading cycle, even though product price goes up.

I'm struck by how the "usership" of appliances and home electronics products in England and parts of Europe contrasts with buying habits in America. Overseas, people are much more likely to rent than to own. Consequently, trading cycles are likely to be shorter. In England, for instance, upscale people tend to acquire new-model TV sets every year or two and then trade them in. The rest of the TV customers can then rent those nearly new models for much less than the sets would otherwise cost.

Actually, everybody benefits when the makers shorten the trading cycle. When as a manufacturer you reduce your customers' trading cycle not only *can* you be more innovative in product design but you *must* be. Otherwise, you take away your customer's incentive to trade with you frequently.

Integrity: Making Money up Front

The customer satisfaction business agenda requires that you be *up front* with your customers and that you make money up front. That's opposed to making money by means that are *hidden from the consumer* on what I call the *back side*. The typical way a business makes money on the backside is through manipulating profits or prices through finance arrangements. A business can use a financial arrangement—either a loan instrument or a lease—to make a profit on the spread between the wholesale and retail interest rates. Or a business can use a lease instrument to give a hidden discount to one class of customer while maintaining a high price to the other class.

Of course, making money on the back side and giving hidden

discounts is not just limited to the retail trade. Any big-ticket item that may be financed—computer systems and office equipment, for instance—opens up the opportunity for large hidden profits on the back side.

Manufacturers need to be honest with themselves and their customers and price products fairly, rather than overpricing and then giving discounts hidden in the financing terms. After all, what happens to you as a manufacturer when you allow yourself to become hooked on hidden financing profits? You become *dependent* on them; and in the long run, you cease being competitive in your product market. Other entrepreneurs will bid those hidden profits away from you by offering customers better terms.

Caught in the Middle

Never get caught in a middle-of-the-road position; you'll get hit by traffic from both sides.

—Margaret Thatcher

Besides being internally contradictory and self-defeating, the gross profit business agenda exposes its practitioners to a newly emerging threat from the outside. For some time now, new competitive forces have been building within many industry value chains—forces that represent nothing less than an all-out battle to capture value added within the value chain. Is this different from good old-fashioned brand competition?

You bet it is. Whereas brand competition pits one manufacturer against another, in the new value chain competition, all the players throughout the chain compete for a bigger share of the final product's value to the customer. Let me give you an example from the auto industry.

For some time now, two trends have been appearing in the automobile value chain. The first involves certain automobile manufacturers—the companies that design, package, and put together the cars we dealers sell. Manufacturers tend to be the eight-hundred-pound gorillas of the industry; they can sleep anywhere they want. As a result, some have been squeezing other businesses in the value chain for margins, both upstream with their suppliers and downstream with their dealers.

Downstream, some car makers would like to turn dealers into service centers; all we'd do then is service the cars. Then the profits from dealer entrepreneurship would go to the car makers. That's one trend, and it's happening in other industries as well.

The other trend has been to a large degree driven by Tasca Lincoln-Mercury. Remember my telling you that the future of automobile retailing was getting baked in right here in Seekonk, Massachusetts? In fact, we've been at the forefront of creating the high-sales-volume, high-customer-satisfaction car retailer of the future. That means we stand a better chance of retaining the profits of retailing entrepreneurship than does the typical car dealer running under a gross profit business agenda. We add value to the final product that the makers can never duplicate, because we're so much closer to the customers, and we know how to satisfy them.

What does that mean for the car retailer *without* our agenda? For that matter, what does it mean for the typical gross profit business agenda retailer in a number of other industry value chains? Finally, what does it mean for suppliers and wholesalers who don't operate on the customer satisfaction business agenda and, as a result, don't capture that value added?

Well, for gross profit business agenda firms, it's becoming more and more like being a vegetable in a Veg-O-Matic. I call it being caught in the "Value Veg-O-Matic." For the unfortunate retailer operating under a gross profit business agenda, here's what being placed in the Value Veg-O-Matic means: From upstream in your value chain, the product makers are grinding away at your profit margins. The manufacturers can do this in a number of ways, both by directly cutting into retailers' sales and service margins and by passing on costs to the retailers that the manufacturers have traditionally absorbed. At the same time, the new breed of customer satisfaction businesses (for example, Tasca Lincoln-Mercury) grind away at the traditional retailers' profit margins by forcing them to cut prices even more. This is the only competitive response to the customer satisfaction agenda their managements know; and by responding in this way, they're practicing *leadership into receivership*.

What's the overall lesson here? In the future, businesses that

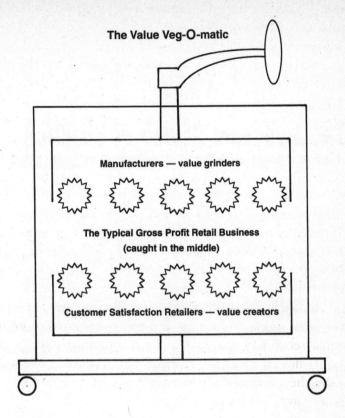

The Value Veg-O-matic

Manufacturers — value grinders

The Typical Gross Profit Retail Business
(caught in the middle)

Customer Satisfaction Retailers — value creators

don't pursue customer satisfaction agendas will find themselves caught in the middle of the road—and getting hit from traffic from both sides. Their suppliers will hit them for margin, and their direct competitors who practice customer satisfaction will create new value, which kills them when they practice price competition. Caught like a vegetable in the value Veg-O-Matic, they'll see their margins sliced away from both top and bottom—costs and prices— until there's nothing left. What's the overall lesson? If you're caught in the middle of the road, make sure you get out quick.

4

The Awesome Power of Simplicity

The Number One Reason for My Success

From the beginning, my dealership's success was based in customer satisfaction. I can remember dealers and Ford executives visiting me way back and asking, "What's the number one reason for your success?"

"Satisfying the customer," I'd say.

"The number two reason?"

"Satisfying the customer."

"The number three reason?"

"Satisfying the customer."

"Well, isn't there another way?" they'd ask.

"There might be," I'd respond, "but I don't know about it. That's what I've always used to make it happen."

You see, I'm 100 percent committed to my customers. As I've already told you, I can't sleep nights if I know my customers are unhappy. I once offered to buy back from my customers more than $250,000 worth of product I knew they weren't happy with. Did they take me up on it? Well, unfortunately, many of them had already disposed of the product, but some did, yes. And we were able to satisfy them.

Most of the time, those dealers and company managers who

questioned me went away dissatisfied. Why? Well, I think they viewed "satisfying the customer," the way *I* defined it, as going to a lot of trouble—and needless expense. They'd rather just sell product.

Once the sale is made, they reasoned, the customer owns the product. Let him worry about it then. Why should *we?* After all, we have enough problems of our own, without shouldering the customers' as well. These visitors to my store would think I was crazy for offering to buy back $250,000 worth of product.

"And they'd be right," maybe you're thinking. "You *are* crazy!"

Well, as I've already told you, *the easiest customer to sell is the one you've already satisfied.* So, in my opinion, the attitude held by those dealers and managers is self-defeating: Satisfying customers is *how you sell product.* That means fixing problems. You satisfy the customer first—even if she's not your customer. Then she's most likely to buy from you—again and again.

Problems Are the Penalty for Living

You see, *problems are the penalty for living.* When you're dead, they'll all go away. In the meantime, what are you going to do about them? This question applies to everybody—not just business leaders and managers, not just co-workers, but everybody in business or in private life. You really only have three choices: ignore them and hope they'll go away, blame them on somebody else, or fix them.

I'm a fixer. I know that ignored problems grow like weeds and that blame boomerangs back on you; blaming causes your own problems to multiply. The only real answer to problems is to solve them; it's like killing weeds at the root. Pulling out weeds before your garden is overrun may seem terribly obvious, but I'm amazed at the number of business people who don't seem to know how to fix problems. At the end of this chapter, I'll give you my simple rules for solving them. Throughout the book, I'll show you how to use these simple rules to make your business run better.

The Engineer in a Coma

—John Pagano, a Tasca co-worker

Bob once encountered an engineer in a company design center who just couldn't seem to understand that customers wanted a different sort of product from the one he was laying out. He didn't want to hear what Bob was saying. The guy just wasn't at all tuned in to the realities of the retail car market. He kept talking about the right way to design the product—which, not surprisingly, was *his* way. Finally, Bob said to him, "You have a problem. Do you know what it is? You're in a *coma*. Do you know what happens to people in a coma? One of two things: either they come out of it or they die. Now, which one are you going to do?"

I think the guy was a little shocked. Did he wake up? I wish I knew.

The key to solving any problem is knowing when you have one. Too many people go through life not even knowing they have problems, let alone fixing them. They only find out when it comes time for bankruptcy or divorce. Let me tell you the simple rule for determining whether you have a problem facing you in your business—or for that matter, in your life generally. Ask yourself: Do I have customers (or friends, or a spouse) that are unsatisfied? If you do, then you have a problem. Otherwise you don't. If you do, find out what the problem is, and fix it. Apply the fix-it rules. Remember, in business and in life generally, problems are defined by dissatisfaction. It's just that simple.

Business Decisions Simplified

Simplify, simplify, simplify.

—HENRY DAVID THOREAU

The customer satisfaction business agenda vastly simplifies a business person's life. Two reasons: First, it means you spend less time reaching a decision on how to solve a customer-related problem. The basic decision is already made: Satisfy the customer! Now, you only have to figure out how. Second, it means you can let your co-workers handle more of the problems you'd otherwise have to deal with. Why? Well, consider the alternative.

If you're following a gross profit business agenda, every time a customer has a complaint you've got to weigh the complaint on the gross profit scale. You start asking yourself questions: If I give the customer some satisfaction, what's it going to *cost*? How little can I spend to get the customer off my back? Am I likely to get my money back if I do try to answer the customer's complaint? How long will it be before I do get my money back?

Most of the time, you'll probably conclude that the best course is to do nothing. Or, you may conclude that the best course is to do the bare minimum—get the customer off your back. Remember what I said earlier, once you start looking at the *cost* to satisfy the customer, you'll never do it. What you *will* do is spend too much time thinking about all the possible outcomes and how they might affect your bottom line. You'll easily become overwhelmed with problems.

What's the alternative then? You can't trust your regular employees to do that kind of thinking for you. The truth is, *they'd rather just take care of the customer*—but that might *cost* you. If you don't do it yourself, you have only one alternative: Hire a manager, and maybe a staff, to do the thinking instead. These people are known as "customer service representatives." Many businesses have them. They get hired as far as I can tell because business people don't trust their own regular employees not to give away the store. The Customer Service Department gets charged with handling customer complaints, usually according to company policy designed to limit the cost of doing so. They're the experts at low-cost complaint handling.

You won't see customer service handled this way at a store such as Nordstrom's. There's a story that is told there about the customer who brought an automobile tire to one of their stores and asked for his money back. Even though Nordstrom's doesn't even sell tires—they're a department store chain—they gave him a refund. L.L. Bean has created similar folklore regarding its customer service, which is rooted in a "no questions asked" philosophy. In Rhode Island, we're the automotive equivalent.

When you hire a customer service department, what have you accomplished? Well, most obviously, you've added greatly to your business overhead, all in an effort to protect your gross margins. What you may find you've done is to keep your gross margins up while your gross sales go into the basement because you're turning off your easiest customers to sell. And, of course, your bottom line goes way down because you've now become much less efficient due to that extra overhead.

I'm told that one of the major automobile companies has a policy that all its retailers must have a customer service representative. I guess they think that's a big advance. I think it's a big, expensive bandage. At the Tasca dealerships, we don't have *any* customer service representatives. Instead, we reach decisions on how to solve customer problems by using the *awesome power of simplicity*. We do just two things: One, we satisfy the customer. Two, we do it at the *lowest possible level of management*. We don't waste a lot of time thinking about cost; we just do it. And we don't bounce all the customer problems up to the owner or the service manager—or to a customer service representative, which we don't have anyhow. At our dealerships, *everyone* has a blank check to satisfy the customer.

You may think this sounds like giving away the store, but it's not. Major expenditures to satisfy the customer still have to get approved. But the problem-solving process goes like this. A salesperson (or service assistant) who encounters a customer with a problem figures out what it will take to satisfy him. (The salesperson should know better than anyone; after all, it's he who dealt with the customer in the first place.) That salesperson comes to one of our managers, or to me, for approval. We ask just one question: "Is this what it will take to satisfy the customer? Are you sure?" If the salesperson's sure, then we say, "Do it."

We don't control our co-workers' dealings with customers on *cost*; we control on *satisfaction*. If a particular co-worker has a good track record on customer satisfaction, we're not going to question an expenditure—even if it's major. And this way, we don't have to go out and gather the facts about the problem; the co-worker closest to the customer already has the facts.

There's another reason why our practices don't lead to giving away the store. You see, if you start with the principle that you *will* satisfy the customer, then from the get-go you'll consider all the potential costs to the customer—not just financial but also emotional and physical—and most of the time, you won't mistreat her. In many businesses, customer satisfaction problems arise because the staff *gouged the customer* and in doing so *created* the customer complaint.

You may still think this is all crazy. If so, chances are the customer satisfaction business agenda isn't for you. Take this book back to the store where you bought it and see whether your dissatisfaction gets you your money back. If it doesn't, the staff may be doing you a favor, because now you'll know how the customer feels when he's not satisfied. If, on the other hand, you find the awesome power of simplicity compelling, you may still wonder how you can possibly accomplish it in your own business life. Read on.

The Tasca Family Commitment: You *Will* Be Satisfied

When I launched my first business, I put a sign up on the building. In big letters it read: "Here We Service You." That's not the same thing as what most businesses say about service—something like "quality service." *Of course*, you're going to guarantee quality service; would anybody guarantee lousy service? The problem is, customers tend to discount those words because they know every dealer promises great service. So, how was what I said different?

In two ways. First, I had us take the pledge. "We Service You" became not just a slogan, but a *commitment*. Second, we backed that commitment up with results that were unique for the time—and still are unusual even today.

Soon after starting my own dealership, to honor the pledge more fully, I had us doing evening and Saturday service; I didn't want my customers to be frustrated because they couldn't get their cars in during the weekday or because they had a problem at night. As I've already mentioned, my co-workers hated the idea at first, and I threatened to padlock the doors—shut the place down—if they didn't agree. When you're really committed to a principle, sometimes you have to make what strategists call a "credible threat." My people believed I wasn't bluffing.

I don't recommend that you make credible threats very often. You have to pick your spots and then be prepared to back up your threats. The only time I use this strategy is when I feel I must keep my commitment to my customers.

Eventually, the word _satisfy_ replaced the word _service_ in our pledge. Why? Because we realized that pleasing our customers didn't begin when they came in for service; it began when they came in for the _first time_, for anything. Sometimes that might be for service; sometimes it might be for the purchase of a car, new or used; sometimes it might be just to browse. So we changed the pledge to "Here We Satisfy You."

When I opened our Lincoln-Mercury store in 1971, I didn't take the Ford store motto down the road with me. I wanted something different, something that would set the new store apart. I also wanted to restate our commitment to the customer's complete satisfaction in a way that would more effectively "sell" our co-workers on customer satisfaction. As I've mentioned, the inside sell is much tougher to make and keep than the outside sell. And the inside sell must be made _first_ and repeated every day; only then can the outside sell get made.

What do I mean exactly by the _inside sell_? If your co-workers are not persuaded that customer satisfaction is important—_the_ most important part of their lives at work—then it won't be, and they'll never satisfy your customers. Customer satisfaction is a matter of attitude and desire more than anything else: It's a matter of _caring_—day in and day out, over thousands of transactions. I wanted to make a corporate family commitment to my customers that would challenge every one of my co-workers every day or night.

Do you know what I came up with? The Tasca family commitment: "You _Will_ Be Satisfied." Later I added on to it, and I said, "You _Will_ Be Satisfied. We'll either fix it, replace it, or burn it. You bring the matches."

By that I meant that anything we couldn't fix to the customer's satisfaction, we'd replace. If that didn't please him, we'd "burn" his old car, so to speak. Of course, to do that, we'd have to buy it back from him first. In other words, the commitment said: "When you do business with Tasca, you don't have to worry; no matter what, we'll take care of you."

We've never had to use the matches yet.

"You _Will_ Be Satisfied" may sound a bit hokey—like some sort of gimmick. But, let me assure you, it's not. One reason is that making this type of promise compels us to live up to it. Blatant hypocrisy is just not something we could live with, nor could most business people, I think.

Also, we know that each time a customer does business with us, he's going to grade us against that promise. Our customer satisfaction ratings at the Lincoln-Mercury store run 9.8 on a 10-point scale; thus, so far, we seem to be delivering. The best part is that satisfied customers eventually tell their friends. That's how we earned that 85 percent preference rating in the Providence area.

I know, and my co-workers know, that to sell a customer in this competitive marketplace, we have to have an edge, something in our story that nobody else has. What we have, and use, is "You *Will* Be Satisfied." My co-workers frequently tell me about the *burden* they feel, knowing that every day they have to live up to that commitment. That they talk often about the burden proves they're truly shouldering it.

Keeping Faith with Our Customers

At Tasca, our customer commitment resembles a marriage. How? Does your spouse like it when you forget a birthday? Of course not. Well, we send out a personalized birthday card every year—to each customer's *car*. That usually provokes a response the first time; customers call up and thank us, and then inform us it's not their birthday. We tell them that the card was sent to their car, not to them. That usually gets a chuckle—and plants a memory seed.

We don't send you a Christmas card; everybody does that, and we'd just get lost. Instead, we send out hand-addressed Thanksgiving Day cards, in which we thank our customers for their loyalty to us. Now, how many Thanksgiving Day cards do you get? Probably not many. Again, our card sticks in people's memories.

Annually, we also run an evening of dancing and entertainment at a local ballroom. Each year we bring in a different nationally known big band—such as the Glenn Miller Orchestra or Artie Shaw. Our customers are invited, and it's all free.

The way we become married to the customer is through *attention to follow-up*; the way we stay married is through *attention to detail*. Follow-up starts before you even buy anything from us. If you're in the market for a car and you visit our showroom, if you don't buy we want to know why. Where have we failed you? Often, that gets us another chance, and we get started on a long-term relationship with you. When you buy a car from us, within forty-eight hours you'll get a call from your salesperson. He or she will want to know if everything is all right and if there's any way he or she can help you further. And you'll be invited to come to one of our monthly new owner orientations. Here, we have you meet your service assistant, the service manager, and members of the immediate Tasca family.

There are three generations of Tascas working in our business now. That shows commitment, too. For a long time to come, there'll be a Tasca around to make sure you're satisfied. The key point is this: When you buy a car from Tasca, you become part of the family. We treat you like family.

You may say that you can't be like me, that you don't have four children and several grandchildren who want to be involved in your business. Does that mean your business can't be a family business?

Of course not. When a person comes to work for Tasca, he or she becomes part of the family. You can treat your workers and your customers the same way. The key ingredient is commitment. I'm committed to my co-workers as well as to the Ford Motor Company.

Time on the Cross

As I've already told you, I run seminars for Ford Motor Company dealerships worldwide. Participants come right here to tiny Seekonk, Massachusetts—sometimes sixty or seventy at a time—twice a month. Recently, a dealer from out west who attended a seminar became very enthusiastic about our business approach. He asked if he could use our motto: You *Will* Be Satisfied. We said yes, but we cautioned him about putting in a firm foundation before he started building a customer satisfaction business.

I guess he didn't listen, because we got a call from him several months later telling us he'd given up trying to make it work. "I got into trouble," he said. "I put menu-price advertisements in the paper, using your formats and just changing the 'sig.' The dealer down the street advertised lower prices and forced me to come down on price. He clobbered me. I advertised 'You *Will* Be

Satisfied,' and nobody believed me. I really got beat up on. Finally, I had to give up and go back to doing business like everyone else."

Before he gave up, he spent time on the cross.

What happened? Is there something unique, after all, about the situation at Tasca that can't be replicated elsewhere? The answer is no. You *can* run a customer satisfaction business anywhere, but getting there takes time and effort. You need to recognize a basic principle: *You can't go from schlock to Tasca overnight.* That dealer out west tried to sell menu-priced product simply on the strength of an ad. It won't work. *People have to believe you first.* To make a menu price stick, you have to personally sell your story—the whole package deal that enables you to deliver high customer satisfaction at low cost over the trade cycle lifetime.

Where do you begin? You begin by building the business's foundation, not the superstructure. Otherwise, you leave yourself hanging in midair, just like the dealer out west. What makes up the foundation? Total commitment backed up by changing pay plans.

Many workers won't like your changing pay plans to reflect a commitment to customer satisfaction. Some will be convinced your intention is to cut their pay.

If you run an auto dealership, you'll see some salespeople quit because they can't make the attitude leap necessary to unlearn all the practices they've used to survive. And you'll see some technicians quit because they can't make the leap to thinking in terms of customer satisfaction rather than getting the job out or beating the flat rate manual. You'll need to be prepared to replace some people.

Next, you'll need to move to extended hours—hours to suit the taker, not the maker—and eventually the team service concept (detailed later in this book) *if* it fits your type of business.

How long will it take to build trust? *Years.* It took us only three months at Tasca Ford, because we'd already built up trust at the Lincoln-Mercury store down the road. If you start from scratch, you should begin to see results in a year. That doesn't mean you'll have reached the end, however. Remember, *customer satisfaction is a moving goal line.* As you're improving, so is everybody else who's practicing it. You need to aim at continuous improvement, or you'll be left behind.

Once you've established some basic trust, you can begin to successfully menu price product—because now you have a *story* to tell that can cash in on the trust relationship that you've built up. Then you're set to go in pursuit of that moving goal line. Otherwise, you'll only spend time on the cross.

Business Lessons in Simplicity

1: **The easiest customer to sell is the one you've already sold.** The trouble you take to satisfy the customer the first time makes your life simpler in the long run.

2: **Problems are the penalty for living.** When you're dead, you won't have any. That's the only way out. In the meantime, if you don't solve your business problems immediately, they'll grow like weeds.

3: **Simplify your customer satisfaction decision making process.** The way to do that is to decide beforehand that you *will* satisfy the customer, no matter what it costs. Then, do it—and at the lowest possible level of management. Now you've eliminated thousands of painful decisions—you've made your business life simpler.

4: **Commit to satisfying your customers.** Run your business for your *customers*, not for your convenience or your co-workers'. Don't let anybody stop you; if you have to, make credible threats that you'll shut the place down before you'll break your commitment to your customers.

5: **Don't spend time on the cross.** If you undertake a customer satisfaction business, build a proper foundation before trying to erect a superstructure. The proper foundation for any customer satisfaction business is the right pay plan.

Problem-Solving Principles

1: **For every problem, there's a dissatisfied customer.** A business problem always causes some person dissatisfaction. When you see dissatisfaction, that means you've got a problem to fix.

2:   **Never place blame; always fix the problem.** Nobody ever satisfied a customer by placing blame. Don't worry about whose fault it is; make sure you satisfy the customer.

3:   **Never be satisfied with fixing only the immediate problem.** Make sure there isn't a systemic problem behind the problem you're fixing; otherwise, you'll be forever fixing the same problems. Systemic problems may be technical in nature, involving either technological or organizational shortcomings. Or they may be people problems, relating to co-worker motivation.

4:   **Never try to solve a people problem with product-problem fixers or vice versa.** If possible, hire people-problem fixers to deal with people problems and product-problem fixers to deal with product problems.

5:   **Never try to solve a problem without the right information.** Get your information first; don't think you know the answer and then go and find information to support your guess—an approach, incredibly, favored by many people.

6:   **Good managers solve problems.** There's only one kind of good manager in any business, and that's one who solves problems. If your managers don't solve problems, you'll eventually lose sales due to the unhappy customers they've created.

7:   **Solve problems at the lowest possible level of management.** Your co-worker who is nearest the problem will have the best information to solve it. Empower her to do so. Make every co-worker a manager.

8:   **The 80 percent rule.** A total of 80 percent of your customer satisfaction problems will (1) come from 20 percent of your customers and (2) be people problems. If you want to run a customer satisfaction business, you must learn how to deal effectively and efficiently with the reality of these percentages.

PART II

The New Job 1: Creating Satisfied Customers

5

Never Gouge a Customer: You'll Have to *Earn* Her Back

You Can't Buy a Customer Back

For years, I ran into car company executives who insisted they could "buy anybody back for twenty-five dollars." They maintained that if a customer wasn't happy with a dealer the dealer could always buy him back by giving him a price that was a little under the competition's. I *know* it's not true. I argued with them for years, and fortunately most of them now understand; the car companies are making large commitments to customer satisfaction.

You see, the proof of the pudding is in the eating. When you try to sell a guy again, he knows how you've treated him before. He's already dined at your restaurant, so to speak. I don't care how low your price is, if he's not satisfied with your service, chances are he'll never buy from you again.

Would you go back to a restaurant that served you a poor meal, if the manager offered you a lower price for the next poor meal? No, of course you wouldn't. You can't buy the customer back with dollars; you have to *earn* her back—and that's a lot harder than if you'd satisfied her in the first place. You see, what makes it so hard is that an unhappy customer will never even come through your door again. Hence, you'll never again have an opportunity to sell her at *any* price.

Never fall into the trap of believing that you can get back the customers you mistreated. It just won't happen. You may think there are enough customers out there so that you don't have to treat them well. Maybe there *are* in some businesses; I'm not sure. I know that there aren't in my business. In today's increasingly competitive world, if I don't treat a customer right from the first visit, somebody else will.

The Case of the Missing Wire: A Detective Story
—Bob Tasca Sr.

A number of years ago, I made a gentlemen's bet with some Ford managers that if I did something simple to partly disable a car, the average dealership would replace a perfectly good part and charge the customer. They didn't believe me, so we ran a little test. I told them to pull an alternator wire off a Mercury—a simple matter to fix, once the technician detected the problem. The car was sent around blind to a number of dealerships in my region; nobody knew that the car was a plant. Every other service manager told the "customer" he needed a new alternator and charged him for one, plus labor—about eighty dollars for a new alternator back then, though they're more now. When the car came in blind to Tasca Lincoln-Mercury, our technicians detected the missing wire and replaced it, and we didn't charge a thing.

Now, at those other dealerships they knew what they were doing: They were detecting a missing wire and then charging the customer for something he definitely didn't need. They were replacing a perfectly good part to make a profit on it. In plain English: They were *gouging* the customer. At Tasca Lincoln-Mercury and Tasca Ford, we never do that; we have designed our businesses in such a way that it can't happen.

MORAL:

Never, never gouge a customer.

The Customer Satisfaction Ten Commandments
Most business people see customer satisfaction as an add on, something to be accomplished perhaps by a customer service department

or representative. As I've already said, that's a bandage in most cases; it'll never work. Instead, I use a set of principles I call the "Ten Commandments for Customer Satisfaction." Some I've already touched on in this book, but let me present them here as a complete set.

There are five negative rules (what you *mustn't* do) and five positive rules (what you *should* do). Everything starts with the First Commandment: *Never, never gouge a customer*. What that means is never take advantage of a customer by making her pay more than a fair price for a product or service. Never make her pay for something she doesn't need.

By the way, don't think price gouging occurs only in the auto business. Anywhere there's an opportunity to gouge, some people will try it—and generally be successful. Look at the construction industry, particularly the home contracting area. There's an old adage that the only honest builders are the ones who go bankrupt.

Now I know that isn't true in all cases; I know there are honest builders and contractors. But let's face it, price gouging happens in this industry, and others. If you're in one of these sorts of industries, you need to protect yourself against the temptation to gouge customers.

There's only one way I know of to make sure the First Commandment for Customer Satisfaction gets followed in my kind of business. That involves how you pay your workers—yourself, and then, your co-workers. Two principles are at work here: *Pay plans determine behavior*, and *Your co-workers will behave the way they see you behave*. The way that you make sure that nobody gouges a customer is simple, and it makes up the Second Commandment: *Never pay yourself or a co-worker on a percentage of a gross profit*. Take away the incentive to gouge a customer, and nobody's going to do it. And it must start with you.

When I first opened my Ford dealership back in 1953, I made a basic decision: I'd never pay myself a percentage of any gross profit made in my dealership. Rather, I'd pay myself a small salary only. By not rewarding myself with a percentage of a gross profit, I avoided the temptation to gouge a customer to make my paycheck fatter. I haven't paid my co-workers a percentage of a gross either.

You might well ask, doesn't this take away all incentive to work harder? In fact, doesn't it stop employees from betting on the come—something you've preached to us? The answer is no; at Tasca dealerships we create incentives that are volume and customer-satisfaction based, not gross-profits based.

The Third Commandment—*Never tell a customer something can't be fixed*—defines much of our service philosophy. If a customer has a nagging problem with a product, the typical service department will brush him off by saying, "That's normal." Around here, there's no such thing as normal. If a customer says she has a problem, she has a problem. And we fix the problem. If we can't fix it, we'll replace it—or give her money back. And we don't make promises to her that we can't deliver. That's the Fourth Commandment: *Never overpromise; always overperform.*

This commandment has to do with commitment and integrity. If a customer knows you're really trying and that you haven't lied to her, chances are she'll be satisfied with what you've done even if it's taken more time and more visits than she would have liked.

People are pretty forgiving, *if they know you are trying and you care*. Remember Avis's "We Try Harder" motto? You know, that motto really worked, for the company and for the company's coworkers. Our motto, "You *Will* Be Satisfied," really works for us, too—though, as I've already pointed out, it places a tremendous creative burden on each of our co-workers every minute of every day.

You see, once you make this sort of pledge, you're committed to living up to it. So, if you're a contractor, for instance, you shouldn't use a low estimate to get the business, and then fail to do the job right. Estimate fairly, offer integrity, and tell the story about your integrity. If the job costs less than you estimated, give your customer a refund. Then you'll have another satisfied customer to attest to your integrity when you bid on the next job.

The Fifth Commandment—*Never worry about the bottom line*—enters into our business decisions in two ways: price setting and satisfying the customer. When we set our prices, we do so without regard to the bottom line. We don't ask ourselves: Are we going to make a net business profit on these prices? Rather, we set our prices in regard to what's fair to the customer, and then we don't vary them.

We don't expect the customer to make up for our own business problems by paying more. That's just the opposite of what many manufacturers, for instance, try to do.

Again, take the case of the automobile manufacturers, and they're by no means unique. What do they tend to do when their projections for new product profits fall short of what they need to generate a targeted return on investment? Invariably, they jack up the prices of their product, because their bean counters tell them it's the only way to bring enough money to the bottom line.

And what happens? The cars are dead on arrival at the showrooms; they're overpriced. Now the overhead costs of running a factory at a less than ideal volume begin to eat them alive. So, after suffering layoff costs and losses, they offer the turned-off customers special programs to bring the *cost* down—not the retail price, but the cost. Too many businesses don't price to market in the first place.

The same thing has happened to certain personal computer and office equipment makers—the IBMs and Xeroxes of the world. They all sometimes forget that the bottom line will never happen unless they first make the top, or sales, line happen. They overprice to "make" a certain return on investment, and then the product flops in the marketplace. Then they have to introduce price reduction incentives to move dead product—at a great marketing cost to them.

What happens to the customers in these situations? They become more and more loyal *to the deal*, not to the manufacturer or the brand. It's all self-defeating, and it stems from trying to manage the bottom line.

What's the answer? *Price the product to market* and *bet on the come*. Bet that you can find a way to sell enough product and become efficient enough in manufacturing the product to make the bottom line happen by the time you're through. The manufacturers often seem to forget the basic rule of finance, even though they're mostly run by finance people: *Sunk costs* are irrelevant in making pricing decisions. The money you spent developing the product is gone, spent; it's sunk. You'll never get it back by overpricing the product to "recover" it. That's bean counter thinking, and it never works. You'll only get it back by selling a lot of product and making a lot of people happy.

Forgetting about the bottom line is absolutely essential if you're ever going to satisfy the customer. The reason is simple: If you ever allow yourself to look at the *cost* to satisfy an individual customer, you'll back off. We don't ever want to be tempted to stint on customer satisfaction; we just do it. For instance, if a customer comes back with a new car and says, "My wife hates the color," we'll tell him, take another one. Since the 1950s, we've had a seven-day, money-back blanket return policy on all used cars we sell: If you don't like it, for any reason, just bring it back. We'll refund your money, in full. If you're unhappy with a service bill, and you feel it's too high, we'll determine with you what is fair, and we'll write the bill down.

How does this apply to your business? You need to take the *pledge*, and then keep it. Pledge that you'll satisfy each customer, no matter what it costs; then do it. Let's say the product involved is a relatively small purchase item—a piece of clothing that's been worn, or shoes. The customer isn't satisfied? Take it back willingly and gladly—and donate it to the Salvation Army.

The next five commandments represent positive rules for customer satisfaction, that is, they're the things you must always *do*, not avoid doing. The Sixth Commandment—*Always treat your customer as custom*—demands you place her need for happiness ahead of your need for front-end profit. You must ask: What does she really *need* in a car? Not: How much car can I sell her? In other words, you need to make the deal *suit the taker, not the maker*.

The Misfit Lincoln: A Story

—Bob Tasca Sr.

A woman called the other day and said she bought a car—a Lincoln Continental—from another dealer in the region. The seat didn't fit her right. She told me that the car she test drove had a seat that was comfortable for her, but the one she bought didn't. The dealer refused to help her. A dealer down in Florida where she spent the winter wouldn't help her either. He told her to go back to the dealer she'd bought it from. The seat had been bothering her for a year. She was angry; she'd spent a lot of money on that car. Would I do anything for her, she asked, even though she hadn't bought the car from me? I said, "Sure."

I researched the problem and figured out that one edition of the car had a longer seat base than the car she'd bought. I had her seat rebuilt to better accommodate her. No charge. It was better, but it still wasn't what she wanted. I priced a new seat assembly for the car; it was going to cost a lot. I told her I would donate the labor if she wanted to buy the new seat—at my cost. I also worked out what it would cost her to trade on a new Lincoln Continental with the seat that pleased her. You know what, she bought the new car from me, and she's *happy!*

You see, what happened is that our reputation for satisfying the customer reached her, and we proved to her that we mean what we say: You *Will* Be Satisfied. And that doesn't mean giving away the store; it does mean treating the customer fairly, even if it costs you quite a lot of money.

MORAL:

Always treat the customer as custom. Personalize her; know her unique needs.

The Seventh Commandment establishes the need to deal with all customers equitably: *Always give every customer the same fair deal.* This means that if you sell ten units of the same product over the same trading period, sell all ten at the same fair price. In that way, one group of customers isn't paying for the other group's ability to bargain you out of a fair deal. This rule also applies to service businesses—home building and repair contractors, business consultants, you name it. When you contract to perform a service, it's always performed in the future. Make sure you end up making the same fair profit percentage from each customer when you're done. If it's appropriate, reduce your billing or give a refund.

The next rule, our Eighth Commandment—*Always take care of your customer at the absolute lowest level of management*—is one I've already discussed at some length. This principle of giving everyone a blank check to satisfy the customer should apply in any store. Should you have to complain to the manager because a suit or a pair of shoes doesn't fit right? Anybody in such a store should be authorized to satisfy the customer—no questions asked.

Be Sure the Customer Is *Really* Satisfied

—Roger Meunier, Tasca Dealerships Parts and Service Director

I had a customer recently who came in with a steering complaint on an older car. One of my service team leaders checked out the car and found that the entire power steering system would have to be replaced. My assistant service manager explained the situation and told the customer what the work would cost—more than five hundred dollars. The customer authorized the repairs, and we did the work. Everything was all right until the customer raised an objection at the cashier's desk. I went over to deal with the problem. I learned that, upon thinking it over, the customer came to the conclusion we were charging him too much. I asked him what he felt was too high; he told me he didn't think the work should cost more than three hundred fifty dollars. It wasn't that we didn't do the work right or that there was some item on the bill he disputed. He just felt it was too much, and he was getting more and more upset. I asked him if he would be satisfied if I wrote the bill down to three hundred fifty. He said yes, and so I did it. After all, I have carte blanche to satisfy the customer.

Later, I found out he went to see the old man [Bob Tasca Sr., or RFT]. The customer complained about the charge, and RFT tore up the bill and handed it back. No charge. The customer walked out without paying a thing. The work got charged back to the service team that did it. It may seem very unfair, but that's the way we make sure we satisfy the customer.

The story illustrates two points: First, you have to make *absolutely sure* you've satisfied the customer. Second, the higher up the management ladder a complaint goes, the more it's going to cost.

MORAL:

Satisfy the customer, at the lowest possible level of management.

The Ninth Commandment—*Always try to fix it right the first time*—should be the goal for any sales or service work done by any co-worker in your business, I don't care if it's fixing autos or fixing shoes. If a customer knows you're trying, that can go only so far toward satisfying him; you've also got to perform, and as a rule, that means getting it right the first time.

Our experience has been that the single biggest reason something isn't right the first time is *attention to detail. Satisfaction resides in the details.* When a job comes back or a customer is unsatisfied when we sell him a new car, it usually can be traced to someone's bad attitude toward detail. We've had technicians we've had to let go, even though they were very good mechanics, because they couldn't get straight how important it is that a car be returned to a customer clean and unmarked by grease stains. The same thing applies if you're a plumber: fix the leaky faucet or appliance right the first time, and your customer will call on you for life. *Especially* if you don't leave a mess for your customer to clean up.

The Tenth Commandment—*Accept getting beaten sometimes*—recognizes that one of the penalties for leadership in customer satisfaction is that some people will, consciously or not, take advantage of you. The only way to avoid this is to treat everybody as though he were a thief—which is how some small businesses operate.

Myself, I'd rather use the working assumption that most of my customers want only to be treated fairly. I'll occasionally get beaten, but in the long run, I know that I'll make a lot more money that way—*and* I'll be able to sleep at night.

The Customer Satisfaction Ten Commandments

1: **Never, never gouge a customer.** Once you gouge a customer, you can't buy him back; you have to *earn* him back. And that's a lot tougher than if you had never gouged him in the first place.

2: **Never pay a co-worker on a percentage of a gross profit.** To be sure you never gouge a customer, never give any co-worker an incentive to do so; pay on volume and on customer satisfaction, but never pay on a percentage of gross.

3: **Never tell a customer that something can't be fixed.** When the customer bought the product from you, he didn't do it with the understanding there'd be problems you couldn't fix. When he's not satisfied, do one of three things: fix it, replace it, or burn it—*after* you've bought it back.

4: **Never overpromise; always overperform.** Build credibility and trust by never promising anything you can't deliver; if you're uncertain about your ability to deliver on a promise, under-promise. That way, if you make your original goal, you'll build up positive credibility with your customer.

5: **Never worry about the bottom line.** If you sell a lot of product and make a lot of people happy, the bottom line will take care of itself. At our stores, nobody ever has gotten reprimanded for spending too much to satisfy a customer; some people have gotten spoken to for spending too little.

6: **Always treat your customer as custom.** Start out with *her* needs, not your needs. Make the deal suit the taker, not the maker. Always factor in what it will cost her. If you're not sure how to treat her, *treat her as though she were your mother.*

7: **Always give every customer the same fair deal.** Menu-price everything. If you sell the same product to ten people this month, make sure each one pays the same price. Otherwise, you'll gouge some of your customers to make up for the profits you lost on the others.

8: **Always take care of your customer at the absolute lowest level of management.** At our stores, every co-worker is authorized to satisfy a customer—carte blanche. My co-workers know that if they don't satisfy the customer, I will, and the cost will be charged back to them, because they didn't do it. The higher up in management you have to go, the more it costs to satisfy the customer.

9: **Always try to fix it right the first time.** You won't always succeed, but nothing irritates a customer more than having to return over and over again for the same problem. We tell a customer who's been back several times and still unhappy that we'll replace his vehicle. Anything to make him happy.

10: **Accept getting beaten sometimes.** When you totally commit to satisfying the customer, you become vulnerable. Some customers will beat you, take advantage of you. You can't let that get you down. You need to go ahead and keep making the commitment and pay the price.

The 2 Percent Rule and the Price Grinders: The People Who Aren't Your Customers

Two percent of the people who come to you, you'll never please.

—Bob Tasca Sr.

I've learned two principles over the years regarding who is my customer. The first is the effort principle: I spend 80 percent of my time satisfying 20 percent of my gross sales dollars. And you know what? Most of the people those dollars represent will never be fully satisfied. Accept it. They're perennial problems; they blossom every season. The danger is that they put into jeopardy the other customers who've willingly paid a fair price and who expect to continue to be treated fairly. You have to put some limits on the problems.

One way is to live by the second principle, which is that about 2 percent of the people who come in the door you will absolutely *never* satisfy. It can't be done. This is true for any business; 2 percent of your customers will continually shop you for price and complain about your products and your service—even on a special price-off program. They are the "price grinders"—the people for whom low price is an all-consuming passion.

If you let them, the price grinders will wear you down until there's nothing left for you, and they'll still be unsatisfied. You can keep your problems manageable by avoiding the price grinders. The best way to do that is to refuse to engage in price cutting in the first place. *Price grinders are not your customers.* Let them go to some competitor who has a gross profit business agenda. They deserve each other.

The Customer Who Wouldn't Be Satisfied

—Bob Tasca Sr.

A while back a customer came to see me in my office. The service assistant who showed her the way said the staff couldn't make her happy and that she wanted to see the boss. I invited her in. The woman said she wasn't satisfied; she wanted a new car. I said, "Before I can help you, I need to know the facts."

Well, it turns out she was driving a seven- to eight-year-old Ford Escort. She'd come in to have an oil leak fixed. We'd fixed it. But she said that wasn't enough.

"You advertise 'You _Will_ Be Satisfied,'" she said. "I'm not. I want you to give me a new car."

Well, I pointed out to her that her car was seven to eight years old, that she hadn't bought it from us, and that we didn't even sell Fords; we sold Lincolns and Mercurys. I couldn't very well give her a new car.

She still wasn't satisfied, though. I asked her if she was upset about the repair bill; she was. So I said to her, "There were some problems with engine oil leaks in those cars, so I tell you what I'll do, I'll charge you only for the parts that went into the repair. I'll pick up the labor myself."

She still wasn't satisfied.

"And furthermore, any time you want to purchase a new or used car from Tasca Lincoln-Mercury, you go make your best trade-in deal with one of my salesmen, and then you come and see me. I'll give you another five hundred dollars off the purchase price."

You know what? She still wasn't satisfied. She still thought I should give her a new car. I guess no matter how hard you try, you can't satisfy everyone.

MORAL:

Some people you'll never satisfy. Accept it.

6

If You Can't Measure It, You Can't Manage It

How Do You Measure a Feeling?

Finding a reliable way to measure customer satisfaction is critical because, after all, the entire customer satisfaction business agenda is based on the presupposition that customer happiness is something you can measure. Obviously, without a reliable yardstick, the agenda doesn't work.

Operating a gross profit business agenda has the advantage of familiarity; everybody knows how to count *money*. Determining a profit—whether it's gross or net—has become a well-refined accounting procedure. I'm certainly not suggesting you throw all that out to operate a customer satisfaction business agenda. Ultimately, we all live or die by what our financial statements tell us. What I *am* saying is that to operate a customer satisfaction business agenda, you need to begin measuring customer satisfaction—in addition to the traditional measurement of profits.

Maybe that's one of the reasons why business people have so much trouble converting to a customer satisfaction agenda: It means thinking about your business in terms of a new and unfamiliar measurement standard. A typical reaction might be: "What, run my business on the strength of feelings? Not on your life!" But that's exactly what we do at Tasca Lincoln-Mercury and Tasca Ford—very successfully, I might add.

In making your measurements, it's not good enough to just measure the _overall_ feeling your customer has—although that can and should be done. You need to _break down_ a feeling into its bits and pieces. If you can't do that, you can't pinpoint _what went wrong_ when customers say that they aren't satisfied. If you can't find out what went wrong, you can't fix it. If you can't fix the problems, then you can't run a business on a customer satisfaction basis.

So, it all boils down to breaking a feeling down into its pieces and then measuring those pieces. Can it be done? Yes. Is it absolutely, mathematically accurate, in the way a financial statement can be? No, but it's close enough that a customer satisfaction business can be run according to the results. Keep in mind, anyway, that accounting is an art also, and financial statements can be made to say what you want them to.

We started measuring customer satisfaction in the 1950s—and we've been doing it ever since. You might say we _invented it_ right here in East Providence, Rhode Island. In the mid-1980s, the car manufacturers began to wake up to the importance of customer satisfaction, measuring it at the dealership level as well as at the product level. Now the Ford Motor Company does part of the measuring job for us, but we still do more measuring ourselves. The big advantage in having the manufacturer do the measuring is that now we can compare ourselves directly to the competition. Since the inception of Ford's measurement system, Tasca Lincoln-Mercury has won the Ford Chairman's Award for Best in Class for Customer Satisfaction _nine years in a row_. So, we know we're pretty good.

Of course, the automobile industry is not the only one measuring customer satisfaction. Customer satisfaction survey forms are cropping up everywhere. Hotels, restaurants, even supermarkets are hopping on the bandwagon. And with good reason.

You shouldn't take these surveys lightly when _you_ shop. They're at the forefront of a revolution in American business. If you register a complaint on such a form, you _will_ be taken seriously.

Measuring customer satisfaction is tricky, because the customer can be _dis_satisfied with either the product or the dealer, or both. Or the customer can have what I call a _people problem_ that really has nothing to do with any of these. What makes achieving consistently high customer satisfaction ratings so difficult is this: *You can do everything right and the product can do everything right, and you can still fail to satisfy the customer, because his problem is with himself.*

Also, the customer can be either pleased or displeased with two areas of a typical store—sales and customer service. So any reliable customer satisfaction measurement must have three components. It must measure the product, the business sales effort, and the customer service effort. When a customer isn't satisfied, that may still not be fine enough to pinpoint the problem, though. You need to know exactly what aspect of the customer's experience on each of these planes pleased or displeased her.

The trick becomes one of identifying the appropriate categories of pleasure/displeasure—categories neither too specific nor too general. These categories then become the common *standards* by which you can compare customer segments in your marketplace and how you match up against the competition.

How do you find out how customers feel about you in each category? You *ask* them.

Finding a True Measure for Customer Satisfaction

Businessmen hate to compete.

—Adam Smith

In the early days at Tasca Ford, our "surveys" boiled down to simply asking people directly and informally. We didn't formalize our categories and mail out a questionnaire until we'd been in business for three or four years. Which brings up an important point: You can't be too small to be able to afford this information. I collected satisfaction data the first months at Tasca Ford when I was the *only* full-time employee.

You can't be too large either. You simply need to make your measurement techniques more formal and orderly as you grow and add more co-workers. The only prerequisite for obtaining customer satisfaction information is a *desire to know the truth.* That can be hard for business people, because they often take what information they glean as *personal rejection* rather than what it really is: a resource. Think about it, if you don't know *why* your customers are unhappy, how can you ever change the situation?

Over the years at Tasca stores, we've become much more sophisticated in our customer satisfaction measurement procedures. We've moved from an informal assessment of customer satisfaction to an independently tallied customer self-report system paid for by us to a combination of our own paid-for system along with that of the Ford Motor Company's. Ford has also been consistently improving its customer satisfaction measurement system since its inception in the mid-1980s; it's much better now, and in a moment I'll tell you why.

Why do we have two systems? Well, it turns out there are some aspects of building a satisfied customer base that Ford doesn't measure but which we've learned over the years to regard as important. *Our* indicators tie together customer satisfaction and our likely success as a store. They appear in the table "Key Customer Satisfaction Indicators for Business Success," and they're readily applicable to any business dealing in higher ticket price products. Notice what we focus on: follow-up and loyalty to our store. Our kind of customer follow-up is impractical for lower-priced products, but loyalty indicators can be used in absolutely any business.

Key Customer Satisfaction Indicators for Business Success

Our Recent Scores

Customer contacted by salesperson within two days after sale?
100%

Overall satisfaction with Tasca dealership?
99%

Customer feels that he can recommend dealer to others
99%

Customer has recommended dealer to others
85%

If repurchasing same make of product, would repeat with this dealer?
95%

Overall satisfaction with service department?
99%

I learned back in the 1950s that a customer whose purchase was followed-up on promptly would far more likely become a satisfied *repeat* customer. It goes back to a basic customer satisfaction principle: If you show a customer you *care*, he's much more likely to forgive you if everything isn't perfect. And of course, the follow-up contact by the salesperson is a prime opportunity to learn if anything's not perfect.

I also learned early on that recommending us to others is a powerful indicator of customer satisfaction—and loyalty; so we ask about that. We also ask whether a customer would repurchase from us, provided he likes the brand. You see, the reason most customers who leave us choose to leave is that we don't sell the brand they want; they want a change in product. Of course, we can't change the product selection situation for them; we're loyal to the Ford Motor Company. But we do want to know whether they'd repurchase from us *if* they were to buy another Ford product. As you can see from the numbers in the table, we do very well on these basic indicators.

What does the Ford Motor Company do? The company originally measured only customer reactions to the product and dealership ability to deliver the product properly. Now, Ford measures dealerships on performance *standards* as well (see Appendices A and B for Ford's sales and service standards. Beginning in 1995, half our overall rating is determined by subjective customer-service ratings and the other half by the dealer's performance against objective standards.

As objective measures, standards apply to every business; how quickly you answer the telephone or greet a customer who walks into your business applies universally. Even if you run an organization in the so-called caring professions, standards can help you satisfy your "customers." For instance, if you run a mental health agency, shouldn't you commit to answering your telephone within a standard time and shouldn't you commit to booking a new client for an appointment within, let's say, two days? After all, somebody's life may be at stake.

Why do *both* ratings and standards matter? Let me tell you about something that I know happens in our industry; it may happen in yours, too.

For some time, I suspected that a few dealerships were *buying* customer satisfaction rating points. How could a dealer do such a thing, and why would a dealer do it? Well, the how is simple. When a customer comes in for the critical first scheduled maintenance appointment, all the dealer has to do is to offer him two things: something for nothing (like a free oil and filter change) and "help" in filling out the customer satisfaction survey form. We don't do that sort of thing, because it's deceitful—and most other dealers don't do it either. First and foremost, when you do it, you deceive yourself. If we fail a customer, we want to know it. But I know that a few dealers do it.

Why? They want to look good with the manufacturer; if they look too bad, the manufacturer will come down on them. You see, the moment a competitive situation gets created—such as the one J.D. Power has created in the automobile industry—some business people will attempt to *cheat rather than compete*. That's why competition has to be policed to some degree. Then it can work to benefit everyone.

The Self-Report Principle

I don't know whether you realize it or not, but all of the customer satisfaction ratings given by outfits such as J.D. Power and *Consumer Reports* are *self-report* measurements. It must always be kept in mind that a survey filled out by a customer will never be 100 percent objective; rather, it will reflect that customer's *relationship* with a product or a retailer. It may be a love or a hate relationship; either way, the subjective relationship affects what people report as things gone wrong. Does that mean people consciously lie? No. It means that the language of relationships is different from the language of engineering. For instance, if your wife screams that she *hates* you, she may really mean that she needs to see more of you, that you're neglecting her.

Let me give you a business example. Mercedes-Benz owners believe their cars are perfect; we know that's not true, but some owners believe it. So, if a Mercedes gives its owner trouble, the owner is likely to ascribe it to the *dealer*; after all, the car is perfect. If the owner fills out a Power survey, he's not going to report some product failures—because the dealer must have screwed the car up. On the other side of the coin, some people *imagine* things wrong with their cars; they come to hate their cars, and maybe their dealers too. Or it may be the other way around: Such a customer hates the dealer, and she comes to hate the car because the dealer sold it to her. Either way, customers overreport failures.

Let's take another example. Suppose you manufacture electric toothbrushes or cordless telephones. How do you handle products that reportedly fail in the field? If you authorize your dealers to make a prompt, no-questions-asked swap for a good one, rather than a return for repair, what's going to happen to your reliability rating from your customers? You can bet it will be higher than your competitors who only authorize returns—even if your products fail more often than they should.

So the owner's relationship with the product can affect the self-report.

How Manufacturers Can Get High
Customer Satisfaction Ratings—Without Cheating or Squeezing

If we say that someone's profits are too *high, we mean one of two things. First, that* the entrepreneur was too efficient. *If he had done his job poorly, his profit margins would have been slimmer. The second thing we might mean is that* he made too many people happy. *A more moderate man would not have tried to satisfy so many people.*

—DAVID CHILTON

There's a general attitude toward customer satisfaction that sees all customer satisfaction problems going back to *things gone wrong* on the product. The fallacious implication is that if the manufacturers focus upon perfecting product, customer satisfaction will take care of itself. Now, if this is true, manufacturers don't need dealers for much—and shouldn't allow dealers to make too much money, either. Notice that this is not limited to the automobile industry; it may hold for makers of high-ticket items generally. This is wrong, and for two fundamental reasons.

First, you as a maker can have the world's greatest product and still have poor customer satisfaction ratings—*if* you have lousy dealers. Or you can have a lousy product and great dealers and get poor customer satisfaction ratings. That won't last for long, though. The dealers will tend to leave you. Either way, you lose. Customer satisfaction comes about as a result of a partnership between the maker and the dealer. This is true for a couple of reasons: First, because satisfaction is the product of a customer relationship, and the dealer is always going to be closer to the customer than the maker.

Second, the whole premise is wrong. You can't build a perfect product to achieve customer satisfaction: It will *cost too much*. The Japanese automobile and electronic companies have been finding that out recently. They put in too much content—and began to dissatisfy their customers on the basis of *cost*. Now, the makers are taking content—and cost—out.

What's the ultimate answer to the maker's achieving high customer satisfaction ratings? *Makers need to make sure that their dealers make a lot of money;* then the makers can make a lot of money, too. Notice that this is just the opposite of the perfected-product sort of thinking, which says, "Squeeze your dealers and put the margins you gain into perfecting product." I am telling you that that will never work. Notice what the argument is really saying: "Dealers—at least some of them—are making more profits than they're *entitled* to, and we're going to take some away and use those profits better on perfecting product." This is typical corporatist thinking, driven by *envy*. Some makers just can't stand it when their dealers make a lot of money.

Why are at least some dealers making profits that are "too high"? Well, there are only two possibilities. One, they are more *efficient*—which means that they are producing more service outputs using fewer service inputs. Or, two, they are making *too many people happy!* Their "product" (customer satisfaction) is so much in demand that people will pay more just to buy it through them. More likely, they are doing *both*. How can either one of these causes for high profits be wrong? Actually, these are the only two ways any business can make high profits. Companies such as Ford and Intel, for instance, make large profits because they operate more *efficiently* than their competitors. Tasca dealerships make a lot of money by making a lot of people happy, and it helps that we're more efficient than anyone else.

How can makers ensure that their dealers make a lot of money *and* deliver high customer satisfaction ratings? When I represented the Ford Motor Company at a J.D. Power customer satisfaction seminar recently, I told the audience—more than four hundred fifty corporate managers—that the chief cause of low customer satisfaction ratings *isn't the product*, it's the fact that some regions of the country are *over-dealered*. The J.D. Power people were stunned. They'd never thought of that. They checked it out, and it's true. The regions that are over-dealered generate lower customer satisfaction ratings than those that are not. Let's examine why this is so.

In an overdealered area, the only thing that most dealers know how to do is cut price. When they do that, two things happen: Their profits disappear and their ability to invest in new plant and equipment disappears as well. New investments don't pay. Right now, I'm sitting in one of the newest Ford stores in the Providence area—and it was built in the mid-1950s! In my area, the stores are old, they're poorly located—and there are too many of them. In such circumstances, most dealers can't afford to make investments in customer satisfaction.

The Old Balloon Trick

—Bob Tasca Sr.

A customer of mine came to me the other day and told me I was trying to cheat her. I was stunned. I asked her why.

"Well," she said, "you quoted me $399 a month on a new Explorer, and another dealer has given me a price of $299, including taxes."

I told her that $299 a month was impossible, even without the taxes. The Explorer she wanted is a $28,000 vehicle. She'd be paying less than 20 percent of the purchase price over the two years of the lease at that rate. Now, no new vehicle is going to depreciate only 20 percent over two years; it'll be more like twice that. She didn't believe me.

Well, she went ahead and leased the vehicle from the other dealer. Later she found out the truth: The $299 a month was for twenty-three of the twenty-four months in the leasing period. The twenty-fourth payment was $3574! The other dealer was using a credit company that would do such a deal—not Ford Credit. Obviously, the customer didn't know it when she signed; she didn't read the fine print. What did she actually pay? More like $449 per month on the average—about $50 more than I'd quoted her. It was the old balloon trick.

What happened? Well, first of all, the customer made the choice to believe a *number* rather than me. She *wanted* the low-ball number to be true, so she convinced herself I was trying to cheat her. Second, the dealer did it to her because we're very overdealered here in the Northeast. A few dealers out there are so desperate they'll do practically anything to make a sale; they don't care about the customer because they don't even know if they'll be around in a few years when the customer trades again. That's what happens when an area is overdealered.

MORAL:

As a product maker, if you want to be sure your customers are satisfied, make sure your dealers make a lot of money.

The same thing happens in the personal computer industry. When a region becomes overdealered, the individual retailer can't afford to give much customer service—"hand holding" it's called. Price competition eliminates the margin that would have gone to cover customer service. This phenomenon occurs in the travel business as well.

What conditions need to exist for a normal dealership to generate high customer satisfaction ratings? Just two things: The business must be *profitable* and it must be *enjoyable* for the owner to run. The reason is simple. The manufacturer or maker can now *discipline* the dealer. If I'm nearly bankrupt, and you, the manufacturer, tell me you'll pull my franchise if I don't change my business practices, I'll tell you to go ahead. I don't care anymore. "Go ahead, buy me out," I'll say. "I'd love it!"

But if I'm a dealer making good profits and I love my business, I'll be worried you might pull my franchise. I'll have a vested interest in being a good customer to the manufacturer. In that situation, if you tell me to change, I'll do it. That's what the makers do in regions that aren't overdealered, and it works.

Obviously, the discipline principle doesn't apply to *all* businesses, but to those in which an upstream supplier has power over a downstream business in the value chain. For instance, companies such as Intel can discipline their downstream customers, because "Intel Inside" is a powerful selling feature for the personal computer assemblers. Generally speaking, high-value-added product makers have at least the potential to discipline their customers.

Are You a Good Customer?

Too many business people spend too much time worrying about their customer satisfaction ratings and not enough time worrying if they *themselves* are good customers. Why is that important? Here's why.

In business, everybody has suppliers. Very often, those firms supply much more than material goods. In my industry, for instance—and in the personal computer industry and many others as well—suppliers do a great deal of the design and engineering work that goes into the final product. You may think of a car as being designed and "made" by General Motors or Ford or Toyota, but increasingly these companies rely on suppliers for specialized design services as well as manufactured components.

Why? Well, take the case of an auto instrument panel or a disk storage drive. A company that makes only such products becomes expert in their design and manufacture; after all, such a company may do hundreds or thousands of such designs, whereas Ford or IBM might only have occasion to do a few. Clearly, in such cases, the specialty suppliers get down the design and engineering learning curves a lot faster. That means they also become the sources for most of the advanced *ideas* within their areas of specialty.

Now, let me ask you just one question. *Who* among a specialty supplier's customers is most likely to get the great new ideas first? The company that behaves like a good customer and doesn't try to squeeze on purchase price or other terms of trade or the company that has a reputation for squeezing its suppliers?

The answer is obvious, but what's the final lesson here? As a manufacturer, if you want to attain high customer satisfaction ratings for your products, you'd better start by behaving as a good customer to your suppliers. In fact, I believe this is a universal rule of business life: If you want to have satisfied customers, be a good customer yourself.

Some Surprising Customer Satisfaction Lessons

- Customer satisfaction ratings are subjective and relational, not objective; ratings don't measure things gone wrong so much as they measure product commitment.
- Customer satisfaction is more like a love relationship than a service problem—more customer satisfaction problems are people problems than product problems; if your customer comes to hate you, chances are she'll hate your product, too.
- The only way to achieve customer satisfaction in your business is for you to want it to happen—it begins with wanting to know the truth about how well you're treating your customers; then you have to act appropriately on the information you've gleaned.
- There are only two ways to make a lot of money in a competitive economy: Either you have to be more efficient than your competition or you have to make a lot of people happy or you can do both.
- The best way for a manufacturer to satisfy its customers is to make sure its retailers make a lot of money; if you try to treat your dealers like service centers by taking away their entrepreneurial profits, they'll bite you back by doing nothing more than they have to: Customer satisfaction is an entrepreneurial activity, not a service activity, and straight salary staff will never make it happen.
- Being a good customer yourself makes it easier to satisfy your own customers; when you behave like a good customer, your suppliers give you their best deals and ideas, which enables you to satisfy your customers more easily.

7

Service Is
the Backbone of Any Business

The Great Quandary: Whom
Do You Satisfy—the Customer or Yourself?

Everybody claims they have great service. But how do you measure "great"? Service can be measured in two ways: great for me or great for the customer. I suspect that, with respect to most businesses, what lies behind great service is two things: profits for the business and convenience for the employees. After all, if you're running a gross profit agenda business, what do you care about? The gross service margin you can maintain. "How much profit can I make on this service job?" is the unit of measurement.

Why do I say that? For one thing, look at the pay plan. How are the employees paid? In my industry, and in almost every other industry with a major repair service component to it, most service employees get paid some sort of flat rate plus a commission based on gross profit. In such a situation, the more you bill the customer, the more everybody makes. Thus the gross profit pay plan has a built-in incentive for violating the First Commandment for Customer Satisfaction: *Never, never gouge a customer.* Also common to gross profit agenda operations is an attitude that views service as a kind of dirty, back-room enterprise—something you have to do but that is really *a pain in the ass*. The real tip-off is service availability. Do service hours get set by customer needs or by management and worker convenience? If the hours are convenient for the management and the employees but not the customers, you know you're looking at a gross profit business agenda in action.

Caught in the Middle

—Bob Tasca Sr.

I had a call recently from another woman who'd bought a Lincoln Continental from a different dealer in the New England region. She'd driven the car south for the winter, where she had a mechanical problem with it—a rather expensive problem. The car was under warranty, but she was told she'd have to pay cash for the repair and then get the dealer she'd bought the car from to bill Ford and reimburse her. Now that should have never happened, but it did.

Well, when she got back to New England, her own dealer refused to accept responsibility for the problem and told her she'd have to be reimbursed through the southern dealer who did the work. She was caught in the middle. The southern dealer took her, and her own dealer didn't care. She called Ford's customer service line, and they said they'd get it straightened out for her, but it would take some time while they gathered all the information. So she called me, because I advertise "You *Will* Be Satisfied." Could I do anything for her, even though she was not my customer? I said, "Sure."

When she came in, I reimbursed her in full. I told her I was sorry for what happened—that it never should have happened and that I'd worry about collecting from Ford. Was she satisfied? You bet. It wasn't my fault and it wasn't Ford's fault, but I took care of her anyway. She brought her car to us for service after that, even though it was considerably out of her way. And where do you suppose she bought her new Lincoln the next year? I love it when other dealers send their customers to me for service.

MORALS:

1.   Never, never gouge a customer.
2.   Always service your competitors' customers.

How are we different? I guess our uniqueness begins with where I started off in the auto business—in a service department as a grease monkey. As I've said a few times in this book, I realized early on that a customer who wasn't satisfied with our service probably wouldn't come back—for service or for a new car either. Service isn't a dirty backroom operation then; it's the *backbone of any business*. You see, the ultimate job for any service department is to *deliver the customer back to the sales door*. And you can't do that unless you make the customer happy with your service in the first place. At Tasca, that's just what we do.

Our uniqueness is evident in how we measure great service. At Tasca stores, we measure it by one thing only: customer satisfaction. Customer satisfaction is all that matters; if a customer isn't satisfied, for whatever reason, we've failed to deliver great service. In fact, our service and sales areas compete to win the coveted high score on customer satisfaction each month, and more often than not, service beats out sales.

However, the difference is so small you could cut it with a knife. Both our service and sales departments regularly score between 9.7 and 9.8 on a 10-point scale, and the winner may win by only 0.01 point. Remember, we don't grade ourselves on customer satisfaction; our customers do. All it takes is just one guy who's unhappy for whatever reason, and a whole team's customer satisfaction score can go down enough to lose the competition. Who ever said competition wasn't a good thing? It sure is for our customers.

In our stores, as I've said several times now, nobody ever gets paid on a gross profit. Our technicians and managers get paid a salary plus a bonus for volume and customer satisfaction. We're one of the few businesses anywhere where a service technician can actually make more by doing *less* for each customer—because part of satisfying the customer comes in keeping the First Commandment, that is, by never doing any work that doesn't need to be done.

A down-and-dirty way for any business person to measure service satisfaction, incidentally, is this: Determine from how far away your customers come. We've got customers coming from such places as Cape Cod—more than seventy miles away. That should tell you something.

Blank Check at the Pit Stop

A man can be a hero in any profession.

—WALT WHITMAN

The way we deliver service here sometimes seems like a pit stop at the racetrack.

—ROGER MEUNIER, TASCA
DEALERSHIPS PARTS AND SERVICE
DIRECTOR

Our service people know they *have to* satisfy each customer; they also know that they have a blank check to do so. We don't give the responsibility to do something without giving the authority to accomplish it.

Don't be mistaken; a blank check to satisfy the customer in our service department doesn't mean we try to achieve customer satisfaction with a checkbook. Obviously, refunding for mistakes is the route to bankruptcy, not customer satisfaction. What we aim to do is to fix things right, the first time if possible, with such efficiency that we can afford to do extraordinary things when we must to satisfy a customer. For instance, a man recently called to say we'd neglected to lubricate his car's door hinges properly when it had been in here for routine service work and a repair. That meant he felt he had to come back again. He was pretty upset. When he came back, we refunded his money—in full. That's what it took to satisfy him. Notice: We don't just make the adjustment for the customer; we ask him what he wants to be satisfied.

Obviously, if a product came from the factory with certain operating characteristics, we can't fix those. What we will commit to doing is fixing what we can cure. In our sales department, we try to make the customer familiar with product characteristics; in service, we commit to making the product live up to its design.

For instance, if a model with a four-cylinder engine tends to be a bit rough running at idle, we tell the customer that. If it bothers the customer, we'll suggest he consider a smoother-running V6. Generally speaking, the more cylinders, the smoother the engine. Now, if the customer finds the car too rough after he's driven it for a while, we can't cure it; but to satisfy him, we'll take the car back and put him into a smoother-running product. We'll charge him only the difference in the price of the two products. That's how sales and service work together to satisfy the customer.

Midnight in the Emergency Room

—A customer

Late in the day recently, I had some unexpected trouble with my Sable. It wasn't stopping right. I was worried that it might be dangerous to keep driving. So, I called the Tasca Service Department. I was told I could safely drive it over to Tasca's, but that because of a heavy workload, they might not get to my car that night.

When I got to the service desk after work, everyone was going at a furious pace. The place was jammed with cars. It looked to me like my car wouldn't get worked on for several days. I'm a single parent and a working mother. I had children to get to school and people to meet at the airport the next morning. I had business meetings and a job interview coming up as well. I just couldn't afford to be without my car.

Despite the work orders piling up at his desk, my service assistant, Mr. Heaney, patiently listened as I described how the car was acting. He wouldn't make me any promises, but he assured me he'd make every possible effort to get my car in as soon as possible. I left the dealership hoping the mechanics could fix my car by midnight when the place closed. My last phone contact with Mr. Heaney was at about 11:15. He told me that most of my car's problems had been repaired, but he still couldn't absolutely promise it would be ready to go before midnight. Having faith, I had a friend drive me over anyhow.

I got to the service department at 11:53 PM. I was amazed at what I saw! It was so atypical of what I've come to expect of American business. My car was the only one still being worked on. The entire Blue Team was still there, swarming over it. Nobody looked at his watch to see if it was quitting time. They just worked furiously. At 12 midnight on the dot, they finished. The hood slammed shut. I was out of there, ready to face the new day. The whole thing had been just like an operation in an emergency room.

MORAL:

Never overpromise; always overperform.

Another key to customer satisfaction in service, as I've said, is hours: We're open ninety-four hours per week, including weekdays until midnight and Saturdays. Heroics performed late at night or over a weekend are just a normal part of how we do business. Our service assistants and technicians become just that—modern-day heroes to our customers. What drives them?

Well, partly it's that our pay plan provides incentives for heroics, but that's not all. It also has to do with the last key to customer satisfaction in service: the team concept.

When you operate on a team service concept, five things happen, all at once. First, you no longer need a service bay for each technician. A good bit of the time, several technicians will work on the same product in the same bay. We operate with fewer than one-third the service bays of the typical dealership—and it's all due to team service. That saves us a lot of overhead.

If I do the same amount of service work in nine bays that you do in fifty-four bays, who do you think is going to make more money? The same principle holds for repair facilities that involve bench work—such as electronics and small engine repair. With team service, you no longer need separate bench space and diagnostic gear for each technician.

Second, when you operate under team service, you replace a loose collection of Lone Rangers with team players who help one another out. So, instead of having a guy really "get in the soup," as we say, and maybe spend six hours tied up on a job that should take less than one hour, the moment a guy gets into trouble his teammates jump in to help. That can really increase the overall output of your entire shop.

Third, when you operate under team service you experience gains from technical expertise. The best technician on each team is far too valuable to waste doing low-level work, which he _would_ be doing much of the time under the Lone Ranger approach. Instead, under the team approach he can spend all of his time diagnosing high-level problems and performing high-level work and assign other team members to lower-level work. That way, through cooperation, the efficiency of the entire team goes up—and the *average cycle time* to complete a work order goes down.

At Tasca Lincoln-Mercury, we complete more work orders per day per stall than any other auto dealer in the world. Period. I should add here that our efficiency also goes up because our pay plan encourages us to follow the First Commandment: We do no work that doesn't need to be done.

Fourth, because we operate more than one team, we reap the benefits of *competition* as well as *cooperation*. Competition between teams for the coveted best-in-customer-satisfaction award each month really *supercharges* our service department. Not only that, because we measure results in only one way—customer satisfaction—we also create competition between sales and service. (Notice, when you make customer satisfaction the common denominator for business performance, you can directly compare all departments in your business—to see which is doing best. Customer satisfaction in fact makes us a *supercharged store*.)

Fifth, the quality of the service product that we produce goes up. Remember, *your customer defines the quality of your service; you don't.*

Team-Centered Service Payoffs

1. **Less space required; lower overhead.** Team service can cut in half, or more, the physical space you need to provide customer service; you no longer need one service station per technician.
2. **Nobody gets in the soup.** When team members cooperate, the phenomenon of the Lone Ranger who gets in over his head and takes far too long to do a job gets eliminated.
3. **Average cycle time drops.** The average cycle time to complete a job order drops dramatically.
4. **Competition improves the product.** Team members cooperate, but *teams* compete; the drive to be the best makes every team better; and both effectiveness and efficiency go up—*measured on customer satisfaction* for the entire store.

5. **Service quality goes up.** The customer benefits directly as repair effectiveness goes up; more jobs get done on time, or ahead of time, and more work gets done right the first time.

Look at the results. An amazing thing has happened, strictly due to following the customer satisfaction agenda for doing business: Program *effectiveness* and cost *efficiency* have both gone up, and at the same time. Now, the business school gurus will tell you that effectiveness and efficiency should be a trade-off: that one can go up only if the other goes down. In other words, if you set out to do a program better, it should cost you more. That rule, it turns out, doesn't hold when you follow the keys to customer satisfaction through service.

Early Morning Pit Stop

—A customer

I recently brought my Mercury Sable into Tasca for what I thought would be some routine service work. I live by my car; it's a company car, and I'm on the road all day most days. So there I was, 7:30 in the morning, sweating out whether the car would be done so that I could make my first business call at 9:00.

Before I'd even had a chance to settle in with a coffee and the morning newspaper, the service manager came up to me and said, "Sir, the work you brought your car in for is finished."

I was amazed. Then he said, "Would you have a little extra time? The brake pads on all four wheels of your car are badly worn, and the rotors need resurfacing. The car needs a brake job very soon."

I had visions of at least a three-hour wait and a missed business appointment or of having to make another service appointment real soon. So I said, "I've got to be in Providence at 9:00 sharp."

"We can have it for you in time," he said. "Let me go over the work order with you and tell you the charges."

I couldn't believe it! He put four guys on my car—one on each wheel. It was just like a pit stop at the Indianapolis 500, or the Grand

Prix at Le Mans. A half hour later, at 8:20, I was on my way. I made my business appointment easily.

MORAL:

Always treat the customer as custom.

What's it like to experience our service facility in full operation? Well, the best expression I've heard for it is that it's like a whole bunch of pit stops at a racetrack—all going on simultaneously. Each of our five "pit" teams may be working together on one or two cars or even three. (Where do the "extra" service bays come from? We do work in the aisles; we do work outside the shop in good weather; we do anything to satisfy the customer—on time.) Each service assistant may be dealing with a dozen work orders and attending to several people problems. Our technical wizard may be racing between teams and cars, helping solve high-level diagnostic problems. Inside our parts department, co-workers race to pull parts to keep up with demand. Things happen so fast that sometimes they literally behave like football quarterbacks; they pass parts through the air to the technicians. If you saw it all, I think you'd agree that *this place is supercharged.*

Customer Service Commandments

Uncaring *gives you [as a co-worker] an invitation to leave. Uncaring is the Unforgivable Sin.*

> —ROGER MEUNIER, TASCA
> DEALERSHIPS PARTS AND SERVICE
> DIRECTOR

So far, we've dealt with customer service here at what might be called the macro level—the level of the total service operation. Are there any rules that you should follow in order to deliver customer service at the micro level—the level of dealing with the individual customer? Yes, there are, and they apply many of the customer satisfaction commandments. Again, these things are the essence of simplicity—in principle. Sometimes they can be very tough to apply in practice.

The first rule in the service department, and I've said it before, is a negative one: *There is only one forbidden word: normal. Normal* is a terrible word. Do you see how that word runs directly counter to the Sixth Customer Satisfaction Commandment: *Always treat your customer as custom?* When you tell a customer, "Oh, that's normal. They all do that," what you're doing is telling him that *you* are the person in the business marriage who defines what's right and wrong. I wonder how many spouses would feel about that one. When your spouse or your customer tells you she has a problem, *she has a problem.* The worst thing to do is minimize her by telling her it's normal.

As I've said before, most problems in service are *people* problems; they're not *product* problems at all. The product problems are the easy ones to fix.

In my business, if a car engine doesn't run, it's either due to a fuel or an electrical problem. It's easy to spot which, and usually easy to fix. In an electronics business, the component is either good or bad—and you throw it out if it's bad.

People problems are far tougher to fix, but we fix them as well. As I've already told you, we hire technicians to fix product problems and service assistants to fix people problems. You might say that our people fixers are our psychologists—except that our "psychologists" don't try to figure out what's wrong with a customer; they try only to fix the customer's relationship with his car and with us.

The Flasher

—Bob Tasca Sr.

Recently, one of my customers brought her car in with a very difficult problem to solve. She said that one of the instrument panel warning lights flashed on intermittently. Her service team checked the car over thoroughly, but found nothing wrong with it—the light never came on for them. Still, she complained about the flashing light. I gave her another car to drive, and I drove her car for several days. The light never flashed on. She was certain that it was flashing on and off for her, though. So we put a recording device in the car, and we showed her how it would record the car's technical fault if she pushed a button when the light flashed on.

Well, she drove the car for several days but said she could never catch the flashing light by pressing the button. We finally had to tell her we couldn't fix the problem she claimed she had with the car. Do you know what we did? We offered her another new car, and we told her we wouldn't charge her anything except for the mileage she'd put on the first one. She agreed, selecting a new car identical to the one she'd had—except for color. So, I have to conclude that she really had a people problem with the first car all along. The color of the car bothered her, even though she couldn't put it into words. I resold that car to a friend and made sure to tell him about the mysterious flashing light. He's never seen it flash, either.

For instance, let's say that a customer comes in with a car that he describes as making a mysterious noise. Now, we could tell him, "that's normal"—but that wouldn't fix his problem; if anything, it might make it worse because then he might "hear" it as being even louder, and he certainly would feel put down by us. So instead we have his service assistant listen for the noise as well. Then we know whether it's a product problem for sure, or whether it might be a people problem—or, in fact, a normal noise.

If our service assistant suspects it's a people problem, he'll still have a technician check out the car. Then he can tell the customer we can't detect anything, certainly not anything *dangerous*. And right there we've dealt with the probable real problem—that the customer feels worried about his security. At the extreme, we'll even take the car back or put him into another one if we think that will satisfy him. We'll also tell the customer to come back if he believes the noise is getting worse. And, we won't charge him a thing, because we haven't done anything.

This leads us up to the second service department rule, another negative one: *There is one forbidden action—doing something that doesn't need to be done*. This is the service department application of the

First Customer Satisfaction Commandment: Never, never gouge a customer. We don't charge to fix people problems, and we don't do any unnecessary work on the cars whose owners have a people problem.

Does this mean we're driven entirely by altruism? Not at all. We like to make handsome profits as much as anybody, and we do. In cases such as I've mentioned here, though, doing unnecessary work can actually cost us. If we did unjustified work, chances are it would keep us from doing the necessary, already scheduled jobs that also produce profits. And in the process of doing unnecessary work, we'd alienate at least two customers: the one we gouged and the one who had to wait for his car. To make sure we keep the First Commandment and never gouge a customer, we don't pay anyone to sell parts to the customer. That's an application of the Second Commandment: Never pay anyone on a percentage of gross.

The final service department rule endorses positive behavior: *There is a need for one continuous action—attention to detail.* This rule is the application of the Ninth Customer Satisfaction Commandment: Always try to fix it right the first time. Ultimately, most of our failures in individual customer service can be traced to lack of attention to detail.

Some people might think we're fanatics about attending to detail; before a car goes back to a customer, it gets checked over by three people: one of the technicians who worked on the car, his team leader, and the service assistant. Even so, sometimes we mess up. When we do, we pay the customer for his inconvenience. Only when the customer is satisfied and the co-workers get paid their rewards for satisfying the customer does the dealership make money.

Notice the order here: customers first, co-workers second, the dealership last. That exactly reverses the order that exists in the gross profit agenda. There, the first to earn money is the business; the employees have to be paid their wage rates, and then they may earn commissions for increasing the firm's profits by selling extra product. The customers come last. At Tasca, the last are first and the first are last. As a customer, wouldn't you rather have it that way?

The Brotherhood

A whisper of a problem is a shout for help. The technicians grow by being part of a Brotherhood.

—ROGER MEUNIER, TASCA
DEALERSHIPS PARTS AND SERVICE
DIRECTOR

When you come to work in a Tasca service area, you automatically become part of a brotherhood. By that, I mean a group of coworkers who care intensely about their customers. Our technicians aren't a loose collection of Lone Rangers who only care about maximizing their individual earnings; they're a really close teams of men dedicated to improving their individual and team skills so as to service the customer better. That doesn't mean they're total altruists or that we've found an answer to the problem of human selfishness. We use the behavioral principles of self-interest and reward incentives to encourage our technicians to work together to help our customers.

How do we do it?

First, we use the basic principle that in a business *behavior derives from the pay plan*. Second, we use the principle that *recognition can become at least as important to an individual as money*. Our service teams compete furiously for the number one team rating. The number one team gets a free Bahamas cruise holiday. It's not the trip, though, that creates the competition; it's the recognition that they're number one. After all, any of them could afford such a trip; they're all top earners. The point is that we use *both* pay structure and recognition to *convert personal gross profit agendas into customer satisfaction agendas*.

Go Ahead: Make Their Day

—Roger Meunier, Tasca Dealerships Parts and Service Director

Last summer at a little before 4:00 P.M. on a blisteringly hot Saturday, a tow truck pulled up in front of our service area at Tasca Lincoln-Mercury.

Behind it rode a small red, well-used Mercury Tracer. In the truck was an entire family, looking despondent—their holiday on Cape Cod seemed in jeopardy. There they were, stuck in Seekonk, Massachusetts, with a broken car, and who knew for how long? The kids grew increasingly fidgety. "Can you do anything for us?" the dad asked, his tone of voice revealing his frustration and disappointment. "I know it's late in the day, but you're the only place around here open for service." His voice trailed off.

He was right; it *was* late in the day and we *were* the only place open. That was just the problem. Our guys had been working hard since 7:00 that morning—sometimes in the direct sunlight. The temperature had reached ninety-five degrees and hadn't dropped much yet. Only one more hour to go, and they could drive home and relax with their families and friends. The service assistant who talked with the new customers looked at his team. "Well?"

The team leader responded, "I don't know; it's pretty late in the day, and the men are all tired, and we don't even know what's wrong with it. . . . Okay, we'll take a look at it."

The word came back in less than twenty minutes. "Bad fuel pump—and we haven't got one in stock now. We just used the last one. Can't get more parts until Monday."

The kids really looked crestfallen now. A couple of the team members eyed them. "Hey," yelled one, "we got a used Tracer on the lot. We could cannibalize the pump."

"Let's go," yelled the team leader.

While they pushed one car and drove the other into the service bays, the service assistant explained the proposal to the family and asked for their approval to install a used part. They agreed. Twenty minutes later, their revived red Mercury Tracer sat happily idling in front of them. Time? 4:57. Time to go—for everybody.

I asked the team members later, "Would you have done it if it had taken more time?"

"Yeah," they said, "it was the look in those kids' eyes. We knew if we did it, it would make their day."

MORAL:

Uncaring is the unforgivable sin.

The service area can't have a customer satisfaction agenda unless each co-worker comes to have such an agenda personally.

Each co-worker must change his thinking from "How much can I make on this job?" to "How can I best satisfy this customer?" And that's all the difference in the world. The pay plan and recognition plan help us *create internal satisfaction* in the service area.

At this point, you might be saying: Tasca, you can do all this without going to team service. That's true. But remember, the team concept also has been designed to foster cooperation as well as competition—and you can't cooperate with yourself.

You might also be thinking that your business isn't service oriented, and there's no way you can apply this discussion of teams. That may be so in the strict sense of the term, but don't define service too narrowly and think only in the complex product repair mode of an auto dealership. Remember, the conceptual purpose of the team-service concept is *each worker being concerned with any customer's problem*. A group of sales clerks in this sense potentially constitutes a service team.

For instance, in a building supply business or a garden supply business, a customer with a problem can be better "serviced" if the salespeople see themselves as a specialized "service team" dedicated to solving these kinds of customer problems. In such a scheme, each team member specializes in one sort of customer problem. In this broad sense, any business having more than one worker can apply the team service concept—by making every worker's pay depend partly on volume, with a customer satisfaction hurdle to get over before any volume bonuses get paid.

But back to the team service concept as its practiced at Tasca. Another advantage is that the individual technicians *grow* by being part of a brotherhood. Let me give you some background.

We began team service at the Lincoln-Mercury store in 1984. We've been developing it ever since. It wasn't perfected overnight; it took years of hard work. Our original reason for initiating team service wasn't that we needed the efficiency to operate in a small space. (When we opened the Lincoln-Mercury store, we also introduced extended-hours service from day one—so we had plenty of service capabilities even in a small physical space.) Rather, we did it because I believed it was the way to better satisfy the customer by *growing* great customer service technicians.

Two principles ultimately asserted themselves in connection

with the brotherhood. First, one way you satisfy the customer is by matching the level of work difficulty his car requires to the technician's proficiency level: *low-level work gets done by lower skill–level technicians.* That way, you minimize the resulting charge—an important element in customer satisfaction.

Each one of our teams originally had four team members; and they weren't all equal. They possessed four skill levels—coded A, B, C, and D—and each was assigned work based on his skill level. One can surmise what the happy result will be, given that no one wants to continue in a low-skill–level job forever; and that highly skilled technicians don't want to become bored and stagnate.

The second principle solves the complacency problem: *Teams provide personal growth challenges for all technicians*—regardless of skill level. Obviously, you could follow the work assignment principle to some degree without ever going to team service; so it's the second "growth" principle that really gets to the core of the team service concept.

As their skill levels grow, technicians within a brotherhood get assigned the more challenging work—often highly technical diagnostic problem solving rather than just wrench turning. They're also required to bail out their lower-level team techs when they get in the soup—and that can pose more of a challenge than if they'd started the job in the first place. Ultimately, our finest technician becomes our technical troubleshooter—the "wizard." He floats among the teams solving the most difficult problems.

In summary, then, the higher-level techs receive the knowledge they're number one, or on their way to number one, in a team. They also compete with the other teams' best people for the number one team award. *But*—they know they can't achieve number one team status by themselves; to become number one they have to help their other team members as well.

That's why in our shop with twenty or more techs working in a small space, *a whisper of a problem gets heard as a shout for help.* Geography becomes a built-in force; geography forces the teams to work closer. *Being number one is the attitude you display when you know you've got a problem.* Some men will do just about anything to earn it.

The high-level techs enjoy a second benefit: the challenge of leadership. *Leadership is never a reward; it is a constant challenge.* You see, these men have the opportunity to become the leaders of their brotherhoods. It becomes their responsibility to see to it that every customer serviced by their team becomes a satisfied customer—in terms of product problems. They become responsible also for their entire team's income and recognition levels.

And yet there is always a penalty for leadership. If a team fails to satisfy the customer, the failure gets charged back to the team. Successfully directing the work efforts of a team demands that a tech develop whole new categories of skills—leadership skills and management skills, not just technical skills. What we didn't see in the early days of team service was that to take on such leadership roles, our lead technicians had to be freed from some of their duties.

Our team service concept really came alive when we realized in the late 1980s that we couldn't expect our team leaders to both perform repair work *and* lead the productive efforts of others. My parts and service director came to me at that time with a radical proposal—that we no longer pay our team leaders a salary based on eight daily hours of personal production against standard.

Instead, Roger proposed that we pay them based on four hours of production and four hours of leadership/managership. We both knew what he was asking—that we take an immediate two-hundred-dred-and fifty-thousand-dollar annual hit against service area profits, nearly one-half of total service profits in fact. But it was that or fail to deliver the kind of customer satisfaction we all knew we could achieve. We simply couldn't expect our team leaders to properly oversee the quality efforts of an entire team and still produce eight hours worth of personal production work to standard. Something had to give. What gave is that we did it—we took the hit up front because we believed it would pay off in the long term.

We did it, finally, because it was the right thing to do. We gave the team leaders four "free" hours per day just to lead and oversee the work of their team members—and we increased the number of team members from four to five. Why did we do the latter? It was simple. We believed that four was the right number of men that a team leader could supervise effectively and cost-efficiently, if he had half his own time free to do it.

Once our team leaders began to lead and oversee effectively,

two interesting things began to happen. First, our customer satisfaction ratings began to go up—and go up dramatically. (On 10-
point scale, we moved from an average of about 6 to an average that
topped 9—all in just a few years. Right now, we're at a 9.7+.)

But the more amazing thing was that, as customer satisfaction
measured in quality control points (QCPs) went up, *so did profits*.
We even changed the meaning of *QCPs* from "quality control
points" to "quality contributes to profits."

Why did it happen? The change vastly increased our attention
to detail as well as our productivity. You see, if you fix it right the
first time, it both satisfies the customer and costs you less. If you're
forced to refix, then it's on the house and you've lost money.

Trash that Attitude

—Roger Meunier, Tasca Dealerships Parts and Service Director

Recently, I had occasion to ask a new technician to take out some
trash at the end of the day; the janitor wasn't available to do it, and we
run a clean ship here. He refused, telling me he came here to fix cars,
not take out trash. I fired him. He tried to get the decision reversed the
next day, but I made it stick. Why? It wasn't the trash per se; it was his
attitude. This is a place where everybody does everything necessary to
running the best shop possible. I took out trash the evening before.
Why shouldn't he do the same? Remember, the *unforgivable sin*
around this place is uncaring. It will get you an invitation to leave.

MORAL:

Attention to detail matters in everything. There is an unforgivable
sin in business, and it's uncaring—directed toward either the customer
or your brotherhood.

The most difficult job to fill successfully in our business is not a
technician's position at all. It's the service assistant's position, and
we *don't* want these men and women to know how to fix cars. We
hire and train them to fix people problems. They are the ones who

interact with our customers directly; team leaders may also, but it's the service assistant's primary responsibility. Each brotherhood works with its assigned service assistant; each service assistant is not part of a brotherhood but works closely with a brotherhood. The team leader and the service assistant together make sure each customer is satisfied. For doing so, they get paid larger bonuses for customer satisfaction. We find that former schoolteachers, for example, make excellent service assistants; they're "people persons," if you will.

Our teams are identified by colors: five during the day and two at night at Lincoln-Mercury. And you know what happens? Our customers become extremely loyal to individual service teams. In fact, some customers brag to their friends that they have a certain team at Tasca that works on their car. Of course, we're not perfect. Sometimes the chemistry just isn't right between a team's service assistant and/or team leader and an individual customer. In that case, we reassign the customer to another team, and the problem is usually taken care of.

When was the last time you heard someone praising a whole service group at a major auto dealership? If you'd like to take a look at the whole picture for how we satisfy customers through service, flip to Appendix B.

What Conditions Are Necessary to Grow Brotherhoods?

As I've already pointed out, the team co-worker concept is not limited to auto dealerships—or for that matter to service departments. Any situation where customers can be better served by a group lends itself to team concept "brotherhoods" of co-workers. Frequently, for instance, sales involves a group effort: create competing brotherhoods of sales teams if your business is big enough to warrant it; create a single brotherhood if it isn't. Do we have the sales team concept in our stores? Not yet; but we may soon. To do so, we first have to change our salespeople's and our customers' *thinking* about the selling process—and that's always the toughest thing to do.

No matter what potential brotherhood situation you're looking at, the principles are still the same: (1) cooperation *within* the team and *competition* against other teams; (2) total dedication to—and performance measured against—customer satisfaction, reinforced by pay and recognition systems; and (3) varying levels of competency within the team, which provide growth opportunities for everyone.

Returning the Customer Back to the Sales Door

Service departments exist for only two reasons: *To satisfy customers and return customers back to the sales door.* Any service department needs to do both, which means avoiding the mind-set that says, "This is how we do business; it's the way we've always done business."

At Tasca, we have two kinds of service customers: Those who are already our customers, and those who aren't. We try to *capture* the future business of the former, and we *compete* for the future business of the latter. In practice, that means following two rules: First, when faced with the choice between losing a customer or losing a profit—lose the profit. Second, when confronted with a customer from another dealership, welcome her with open arms. That's how we both *capture* the market and *compete* in it.

You know, I just love it when my competitors' customers come to me for service. They ask us if we'll service them, even though they didn't buy the car from us; we say, "Sure!" Who do you think they'll buy their next car from—their present dealer or us? We'll service you no matter who you bought your car from—no questions asked.

We're really helped by the attitude expressed by a few dealers: "You bought it from Tasca, you go have Tasca service it." I just love it when they say that. When I hear that conversation relayed, I know we'll have another customer—for life. After all, how have *you* felt when that's been done to you? In *any* business (for example, the farm implement business, where immediate service can save a whole crop) you need to look at a service request from someone who's not your customer as a golden *opportunity*—not as an unfair request or as a pain in the neck.

My *overall marketplace strategy* is to *capture the market where it's mine; compete where it's not.*

Customer Service Principles

- **Service is the backbone—not the backroom, of any business.** If you don't service the customer right—ideally, on the first visit—he'll never come back to you again, and you'll never get the chance to sell him again.
- **Great service is measured by customer satisfaction, not by gross profits.** A gross profit business agenda will never yield customer satisfaction; the only way to measure great service is by customer satisfaction—and that means adopting a customer satisfaction business agenda.
- **Pay plans determine behavior.** If you want your co-workers to satisfy your customers, give them a pay plan that rewards them for doing so, not a pay plan that rewards them for gouging customers.
- **Sales opens the door; service keeps it open.** The job of the service department is to deliver the customer back to the sales door.
- **The hours your service department are open tell whether you're dedicated to customer satisfaction or not.** If you're not open when your customers need you, you're dedicated to satisfying yourself, not your customers.
- **Use the gains from efficiency to pay for the real costs of giving customer satisfaction.** If you can get efficient enough, customer satisfaction in service becomes *free*—for everyone.
- **Employ a brotherhood, not a bunch of Lone Rangers.** When your service technicians work together, efficiency goes up and average cycle time to complete a work order goes down; then everybody's happy.
- **Use great customer service both to capture the future business of present customers and to compete for business that you don't yet own.**

8

Never Cut a Price: Content Can Beat Price Every Time

The Life Saver Sable: A Story

Several years ago, shortly after the government mandated driver-side airbags, we saw an opportunity out there in the market. As I've already mentioned, we believed that the public really wanted the security of both antilock brakes and *dual* airbags—that is, airbags to protect both the driver and front seat passenger. You may remember that the Ford Motor Company pioneered the inclusion of safety-related content in automobiles way back in 1956—and at that time Ford got wiped out in the marketplace. Nobody wanted seat belts or the other safety features Ford pioneered.

What had changed since 1956? Well, we'd learned a lot more as an industry about how to reduce accident-related injuries, and the public had slowly changed its basic beliefs about automobile safety. In 1991, at Tasca Lincoln-Mercury we believed that people's changed beliefs were creating an opportunity for us.

You see, at that time very few new automobiles offered both antilock braking systems and dual airbags—"bags and brakes" we called them—and they were all very expensive; the common person couldn't afford them. We gambled that people really wanted them on an affordable car; in other words, *we bet on the come*. What did we do? We ordered *all* of our Mercury Sables with both features—hundreds of cars.

How was that a gamble? Well, all of our competition in the Sable car category ordered product only with the *mandated* content—driver-side airbags. The result: We had the only affordable, regularly stocked products in the local marketplace with dual airbags and brakes. We were also more than one thousand dollars higher in price than anybody else in the marketplace! So how did we sell that additional content when we were overpriced in a price-sensitive market?

We told a story. The story line was this: At Tasca, we care about your *safety*. We ran television ads showing the difference in an accident between a car with and without airbags. When people came into our dealership, our salespeople told them the same story. Everybody sang from the same song sheet. We also captured people's minds with a short, memorable catch phrase—something that became the story we were telling. We used it on television, in print, and in our personal selling story. What we came up with was this: "The Life Saver Sable," and to reinforce the concept we put a roll of Life Savers candy on the dash of each automobile. I don't know why we didn't get sued by the company that owns the Life Savers brand, but we didn't.

Did it work? You bet. We sold more Sables than the seven local Ford dealers combined sold lower-priced Tauruses. We outsold every mid-priced brand in the local market. It was one of the most successful promotions we ever put together. We did very well by doing good for our customers.

And we drove our competitors nuts. Most of them responded the only way they knew—they cut their offering prices to customers even further in an attempt to make up for our higher content.

Of course, we make it a policy to menu-price our cars. That meant our average deal was running some three thousand dollars higher in this car category. Even so, we still outsold the competition, and some of them probably lost money on the units they moved. Eventually, of course, our competitors wised up and began ordering similarly equipped product. But, by then, we'd already moved on to something else.

Leadership into Receivership

All too often, business people come to believe that the only way to compete—especially against the large retail chains—is to cut their prices. Remember, *anybody can cut a price;* it's the easiest marketing ploy. It's also the most disastrous. We have a saying around here: Never cut a price; always raise content instead, and if possible, cut *cost* to your customer. You see, when you cut a price, all you are doing is practicing what I call *leadership into receivership.* A lot of auto dealers and other business people during this last recession went bankrupt for exactly that reason; all they knew how to do to move product was cut price. That's not the kind of leadership that you want to get yourself into. Instead, you want to practice leadership in customer satisfaction.

You have to understand the fundamentals of how the marketplace works, and the fundamentals are true for any business you happen to be in. Only two things sell product: content and price. It's just that simple. That's all you have to work with directly. If you have product that isn't moving fast enough, raise the product's content—never just cut your prices. The reason the product isn't moving is that the content doesn't sparkle enough to capture the customers' fancy—and cutting a price will never, never fix that.

How do you add content, you might ask, when you already have the goods in the store? Don't you have no choice but to cut price then? The answer is no. You've already read the story "Six Hundred Strippers." There are many subtle ways to add content.

Do you have a women's apparel line that's dead on arrival? You may be able to alter it or add to it. For example, via accessories that complement it. Glitz it up, if that's what the customer wants, or tone it down. Make it come alive to the customer. If *you* can't figure out how to do it, pay your salespeople a small volume bonus to move the product; then most likely one of them will figure out a way to boost the content.

Incentives Create Creativity in Selling

You can also add content indirectly to the product by changing how you serve your customers (change the hours that you're open, for instance) or by lowering the cost of use to your customers (fix it or replace it at no charge if something goes wrong, for instance).

Content, then, is anything that increases the perceived value of your offering to the customer. The point is this: There are many ways to raise product content, and they're all preferable to the one way to practice leadership into receivership: cutting a price.

Content and Cost Versus Price

We're the McDonald's of the retail auto industry.

—BOB TASCA SR.

Let's dig a little more into marketplace principles. You already know that content and price sell product. You also know the principle that low price goes away the moment the customer walks out your door—although you may not yet fully understand why. Low price can never be the road to customer satisfaction. Only high content at a fair price will create satisfied customers—customers for life. Remember, people don't get upset because they paid too much in the abstract; they get upset when they think they may have paid *more than somebody else*. "More than somebody else" defines an unfair price. Now what you may not know is that a low price may contain *hidden costs* to the customer. That hidden cost may cause a customer to pay more than somebody else—even when the purchase price is lower.

You see, too many business people only know their own *purchase* cost for the product; they never even think about what the product really costs the customer. Price and cost are not the same thing; a low price *contains* hidden cost, and that's why it's low. What are some of the hidden costs of ownership buried in a low price? They potentially include high financing costs, lack of "creature feature" content ("the product was cheap, but I hate it"), poor product service, inconvenience, and ownership risks. Remember, a new product becomes a used product the moment you walk out the door with it. That's another marketplace principle. It's now worth less, usually much less. The attraction of that low price goes down accordingly. The value of high content and low post-purchase cost to the customer, however, can last a lifetime. What's the principle? *Any time you can both reveal and eliminate hidden cost for your cus-*

tomers, they'll love you for it—and they'll pay you a fair price for what you've given them. In the long run, you'll make back more than the costs you've incurred.

At Tasca, we say we're the McDonald's of the retail auto industry: We sell at menu prices just like McDonald's (you don't come in to bargain over the price of a Big Mac), we're open hours to please our customers, and we use the finest ingredients. Well, let's apply these marketplace principles to McDonald's itself. Let's say that McDonald's has a product line that's not selling well; what should management do about it? Cut the price? That might move more of the product, but look at the *harm* it would do to the business. It would merely cause people to substitute the slow-moving product for a more expensive McDonald's product that they would rather buy—except for the low price. What occurs when management cuts a price? The business loses profits and the customers become less satisfied—because the low price goes away by the time they've eaten the less appealing product. Their stomachs might be grumbling enough to switch to Burger King instead.

What *should* be done? Fix the content problem and keep the price the same or raise the content and the price. Now you could do this in two ways. You could fix the content in a way that keeps your business costs low—add salt or sugar to enhance flavor, for instance. But that increases the hidden cost to the customer—the cost of poor health. (This is a cost, incidentally, that more knowledgeable customers actually might discern.) An alternative is to fix the content problem creatively by adding herbs or healthy spices that enhance product appeal and don't cost the customer health. Then you might follow up by letting the world know the difference, telling your new product's story and possibly giving it a new name. In other words, flaunting it.

I suppose the classic example of content literally beating price every time comes from Proctor and Gamble. Those people have known for years that if you offer a container with more shampoo in it—a so-called economy size—for a lower price per ounce, customers will use more each time they shower and feel happy doing it. It *costs* them no more. They may even reduce the time taken to use the product up—and buy more from you than if you hadn't offered them the "economy size." You probably will gain volume through increasing your market share. If, instead, you'd cut your price to move more product, your customers may have taken the lower price to mean lower quality—and shifted their allegiance to a competitor's brand. Cutting a price can be disastrous to your business prospects.

Price and Content Principles

- **Any time you can raise content and lower customer cost at the same time—do it.** This defines "opportunity" for a customer satisfaction business.

- **Higher content and lower customer cost validate a price.** High content, lower customer cost situations give you a franchise to raise your price. That's how you as a business person benefit from the value you create for your customers.

- **Your sales staff shouldn't do arithmetic; they should tell a story.** Too many salespeople end up being pencil and button pushers. They spend most of their time doing arithmetic, figuring out the highest price that the customer can pay. Do you know what that does? It not only diminishes the time they have to treat your customer as custom, it positively *kills* your chances of them making a sale. A good salesperson spends most of his or her time understanding the customer, demonstrating the product, and *telling your story.*

A Business Like an Elephant: We Never Forget You

We follow the customer until he either dies or buys.

—BOB TASCA JR.

So far, I've told you how to use stories to communicate high content and low cost to your customers and how to avoid leadership into receivership—ruinous price cutting. But you might well ask, what if after you've told your story, the customer *still* doesn't buy? What if, instead, she walks out the door?

If this is the first time she's visited your shop, don't be surprised.

You see, in any big-ticket–item business, a new customer is highly unlikely to buy the first time.

Think about it this way. In the traditional automobile dealership, what percentage of interested buyers who enter the showroom for the first time actually go on to buy a car from that store? For that matter, how many interested customers who enter *any* business that sells big-ticket items actually buy? The answer is under 20 percent—well under.

At Tasca, though, we sell 60 percent of those first-time potential buyers. In other words, we sell more than *three times* as many serious prospects as do traditional dealerships or other big-ticket–item stores in product classes such as jewelry, personal apparel, yachts, or private aircraft—even though we refuse to bargain on price. The secret to our success involves *how we treat the customers who don't buy from us after the first visit.*

You see, we realize that many first-time visitors still believe they need to go through the ritual comparison shopping and competitive bargaining game. They don't *trust* us yet. And, they don't want to feel pressured; that's what turns a lot of people off about car dealers—the pressure to buy right away. We don't pressure people to buy. Instead, we do two things most stores don't do: We *greet* prospective buyers before they ever encounter a salesperson, and we *follow up* on every potential buyer who hasn't become an actual customer. I've already told you the result: we actually sell 60 percent of those potential buyers who don't buy after the initial visit.

How many do the typical auto store sell? Practically none. That's the difference. In other words, "*We follow the customer until he either dies or buys.*"

How do we make it happen? We start with some people I've mentioned before, our greeters. I call them our "maitre d's," because they enable us to treat our customers much the way fine restaurants do. I also call them our "goodwill ambassadors." We wouldn't even think of running a store without them. We don't want their work to be high pressure; we want it to be *high quality*. The people we hire as greeters are totally people oriented; they love people and love to relate to them. One of our greeters, before "retirement," used to be an immensely popular local talk-show host. The greeters in our two stores are absolutely critical to our success—at least as much so as our salespeople and service technicians. Why?

Well, let's begin with a fact of life about auto dealerships: Most people *hate* to enter them. They fear that they're going to get taken somehow. And you know what? They're sometimes right. So, our greeters work to overcome the stigma that has been unfortunately, and often unfairly, attached to our industry. They put the potential customer at ease and begin to create a relationship with the customer built on trust.

Second, our greeters determine the best likely match between the new customer and the available salespeople. They *know* people; they know what salesperson to match up with a pipe smoker, for instance. Most new potential customers whom you lose are lost not because the customer didn't like the product or the deal, but because *they didn't connect with the salesperson*. Last, the greeters obtain the necessary follow-up information on each customer, which gives us as business people an accurate track on what went on in our showroom as well as the basis on which to actually do follow-up.

Notice, we don't rely on our salespeople to log customers, and we don't leave it just to the salespeople to follow up on potential buyers, either. Why? Well, salespeople, unfortunately, tend to log only the people who appear promising to them; as a result, relying on the sales staff will mean forfeiting at least half of your potential buyers. Also, salespeople tend to *pursue* only those people who appear promising to them.

Salespeople's suppositions about who should be logged and pursued are an example of what I call *playing God* in business, and it almost always hurts you. You *don't* know who will buy. The people who have a problem with the salesperson will then get lost. So, we assign logging to our greeters, and we assign follow-up to specialists who attempt to make the connection with us happen. What these co-workers do is find out *why* people didn't connect with us. Usually, it turns out that for some reason or other, they didn't like the salesperson; the personal chemistry just wasn't right. In that case, we reassign them to another salesperson.

Together, our greeters and specialized follow-up co-workers constitute our customer control activity. We learned a number of years ago that we could lose track of customers if we didn't create a system to help us never forget them. In fact, we found we had a *system* problem that caused us to lose customers when we occasionally had a salesperson leave us for some reason; through this experience we learned how important our sales staff is to our customers. When the customers got lost; they became *orphans*. Now, we have a system to help our salespeople and make sure we never forget.

The Orphans

—Bob Tasca Sr.

A number of years ago we at Tasca met with a disturbing number of complaints about customer satisfaction. Each time a complaint arose, we'd assign someone in either sales or service to deal with the unhappy customer. Each time, we eventually managed to satisfy her, but we kept getting complaints that we didn't expect. There didn't seem to be any pattern to the complaints; they weren't all the same product problem, and they weren't generated by the same co-worker. Some of them were people problems and some were product problems. We were confused. Why were we getting so many seemingly random complaints?

Eventually, one of us figured it out: *All of the complaints originated from customers whose salesperson had recently left us.* We'd had several unfortunate situations in which some of our most valued salespeople had gotten ill or had died. And we didn't realize at first what had happened to their customers: *They'd become orphans.* They felt abandoned, and because they couldn't put into words their feelings, they acted them out; they found fault with our routine dealings with them.

You see, we hadn't realized how important a salesperson, or for that matter a service person, can become in a business dedicated to customer satisfaction. A large part of customer satisfaction comes through the relationship our customers build with our people—especially our sales staff and assistant service managers. When that relationship was abruptly broken—through no direct fault of our own—we wound up with very unhappy customers. We had a *system* problem that we had never imagined possible, and the system problem caused a lot of people problems.

How did we *solve* the people problem? We created an "orphan department" within our main office and assigned one co-worker to work with orphan customers, until they could be carefully reassigned to another salesperson. That fixed the problem. And we still do it today.

What happens to the customer who shops us and doesn't enter into a purchase process? He or she gets a letter signed by me personally asking *What did we do wrong? How did we fail you?* He or she also gets a telephone call from one of our specialists. The call is never a high-pressure sell; it's always aimed at finding out what went wrong. Then the specialist attempts to get the person to give us another chance to make her satisfied. Does it work? Well, as I've already told you, we convert 60 percent of these people into customers. I'd call that success.

Our approach to getting and keeping customers is summarized in something we call the Eleventh Commandment for Customer Satisfaction—*Marry* your customer, until *debt* or *death* do you part. You know, most families have a physician and a dentist—maybe even a grocer or a fish dealer. At Tasca, our attitude has always been, why shouldn't they also have a family car dealer? Or a family dry cleaners or shoe repairer for that matter? *Any* business can become wed to its customers for life. You simply need to keep the Eleventh Commandment and desire always to keep your customers happy.

Will you always succeed? No, just as in any marriage. But never, never break your commitment.

Promoting Your Story

One-half of our advertising money is wasted, but we don't know which.

—OLD ADAGE

Many people assume that our success lies in advertising—either that it's unique or that we use a lot of it. Well, I can tell you right now, that isn't so. We don't win by *outadvertising* the competition; we win by *outsatisfying* customers. We've always been successful with our advertising in terms of generating *traffic*. And when we use advertising to generate traffic through a promotional *story* such as the "Life Saver Sable," we do very well. Generally speaking, though, we find that advertising is growing less and less effective.

Back in the 1960s, we started running advertising promoting the "Tasca 300"—a play on our racing reputation in which we told the public that we would sell three hundred new cars in a short time. We still do that today, but we find that the heavy promotions don't generate as much in traffic as they did in the 1980s when the car market was hot. People are simply *allocating their money differently today*, and we have to compete for it against home-related merchandise as well as competing makes of automobile. Of course, that's true for most retailers as well; the auto industry isn't unique in this regard. We could sell as many cars today as we did in the heydays, but we'd spend too much on promotion to generate the necessary traffic. It wouldn't be cost effective.

When we do advertising, we've found it's best to use a very simple idea—such as "Renew Every Two." We do both product price ads and product endorsement ads—but the message is always very simple. For instance, last February we ran a Washington's Birthday advertisement that really helped us sell a lot of cars. Bob Jr. hit on the idea. It just so happened that the way we equip our menu-priced cars plus Ford's dealer programs allowed us to offer three of our most desirable Lincoln-Mercury offerings all at the same lease rate—$299 per month, no money down. At that identical price, we could make our usual fair profits on all three products. So, we advertised the three products, and then gave the single price—in bold numbers. Wasn't that competing on price, then? No. We didn't cut our price; we used price *similarity* to emphasize *value*. The ad really worked. Of course, we always advertise the story that never changes—"You *Will* Be Satisfied."

Do you know the biggest mistake most business people make when it comes to advertising? They use a rule of thumb that links advertising to sales—as though advertising *caused* sales. Advertising usually doesn't *cause* sales; it's merely *related* to sales, and there's a world of difference. Let me explain. In our industry, for instance, a car retailer may decide up front to allocate to advertising several hundred dollars per product unit that he wants to sell in the future. He does it, because he's always used that rule of thumb in the past.

But in reality, he may be spending too much—and merely wasting advertising money and traffic, rather than creating sales. Using such rules of thumb almost always leads to overexpenditure and a false reliance on advertising. You see, in most businesses, advertising doesn't generate sales; it generates *traffic*. It's then up to your co-workers to make the sales happen.

So, when you use advertising to promote your story, use a quantity of it that will ensure you as much traffic as you need to produce the number of prospects you need to yield the number of sales that you want to make. To make it all happen, you need to use the Lombardi principle—break your sales game down into its components, estimate the percentages for each component, and then play the percentages. The critical percentage here is *closing ratio*. How many prospects in your industry can your sales staff close? Make sure that you make your closing ratio happen. Then work all the numbers back from there, and you'll know how much to spend for traffic to promote your story.

Putting It All Together: Volume-Selling Principles

- **Package product.** Determine the high content–low cost package(s) that will be best for your customers.
- **Bet on the come.** Buy in a lot of those products; remember, if you don't buy a lot, you'll never flourish.
- **Menu-price product.** Sell every customer at the same fair price that allows you to make profits one slice at a time; never cut a price.
- **Tell a unique story about your business.** Never talk low price; always name the unique benefits that you offer the customer; tell a story, don't do arithmetic; and if possible, make the packaged product and its story relate to an opportunity in the marketplace.
- **Make your pay plan conform to the sales agenda.** Set pay incentives to reward co-workers for satisfying the customer and selling in volume—not for gouging the customer.
- **Make the first repeat sale happen.** Find a way to make your customers come back to you for the first repeat sale. After that, selling becomes easy. Remember, the easiest customer to sell is the one that you've already sold—and satisfied.
- **Make it all happen.** It'll never happen if you sit back and wait for

it; if you try to make it happen and fail at first, at least you'll be failing forward, and eventually, you'll win.

- **Pay for traffic, not for sales.** When you promote the story you use to make it happen, don't waste money overadvertising: Know the percentages in your entire selling process, and pay for only enough advertising to generate the traffic you need to make your selling process work.

- **In everything you do, remember to always keep the Eleventh Commandment:** Marry your customer—until debt or death do you part. Always follow up on every potential new customer; don't pre-judge who'll buy—*don't play God.*

9

Waking Up the Dead

Story Telling

You can have the greatest product in the world, you can even have the nicest store around, but if you don't tell anybody about it, you'll never prosper. Conversely, if your product is dead in the marketplace, you can bring it back to life by, first, fixing the product if it needs fixing and then creating a story to make the product come alive. Nothing can beat the power of a simple but compelling story.

And don't think of story as being something only for your customers, a slogan or catchphrase; your business's story is more important for your workers than for your customers—because ultimately only your workers can make your story become real for your customers.

That was true for "Quality Is Job 1." I got that story adopted at Ford—not for our customers only, but for Ford workers as well. You see, I knew that each assembly-line worker had to make quality his or her own job 1, or the customer would never see high quality in a Ford product. Who do you think "We Try Harder" was really for—you the customer or Avis workers? Think about it.

At Tasca, we have two stories that we always tell customers: the story that never changes and the story with which we presently promote sales. The story that never changes is "You *Will* Be Satisfied." We tell prospective buyers *why* they should buy from us: We're open hours to please you, not us; our co-workers have a blank check to satisfy you; we'll do anything it takes to make you happy; we give you more content for less *cost* to you; if you find you don't like the color or the model, take another one; return the used car you bought from us within seven days, and we'll give you your money back—no questions asked.

The story that never changes establishes the permanent basis for our uniqueness—and for why you should consider a long-term relationship with us.

We also tell you a story that explains why you should buy from us *now.* This story changes frequently to meet opportunities in the marketplace—it's opportunity focused, and we use it to bet on the come.

What's the lesson here? If you're a manufacturer, you need to create a powerful story to invigorate your product's life. If you're a retailer or a wholesaler, don't leave effective story up to the product's maker. The "Lonely Maytag Repairman" is a great story, but it won't make your cash register ring day in and day out. When the manufacturer doesn't make it happen, you have to. Let me tell you about some of the ways we've made it happen at the Tasca stores—ways that involve creating hot product from cold ingredients and then telling a story about it.

Waking Up the Product

The first story we hit on was "Only at Tasca's." The strategy was the custom car. Obviously, if we could create a unique product for the customer, he could buy it only from us, so we could easily sell a lot and charge a menu price for each one. That's what we've been doing now for thirty-five years. How do we *make it hot to sell a lot?* We find an opportunity in the market to sell the custom product for a moderate cost to the customer by "making" it for a low cost to us. We call this strategy *"waking up the product."* We take a product that the maker has put low content into and we add in exciting and unique new content—at a low cost to us. As a result, the product comes alive on the sales lot.

You know what? It worked thirty-five years ago, and it still works today. "Six Hundred Strippers" and "The 'Mercury-Benz'" are just two such stories, out of dozens, that we've successfully sold. We're waking up a product right now, even as I talk to you.

Are cars the only products that can be brought back to life by an enterprising business person? Certainly not. Consider, for instance, what the Founder of Dell Computer did while he was in college. He took stripped-down IBM personal computers and "souped" them up with simple plug-in components. Then, he sold his souped up computers to his friends—at a fair price. He made a lot of money *and* he made all his friends happy. More important, he embarked on an incredible business success story. Look around for an opportunity in your business to wake up the dead.

The "Mercury-Benz"

—Bob Tasca Jr.

The Ford Motor Company introduced a new product line in the mid-1970s: the Ford Granada-Mercury Monarch series. The press releases on these cars ballyhooed their design, which was meant to make them resemble a Mercedes-Benz. The resemblance didn't go very far. They were still very "American" in appearance, and the typical car dealer sought to increase his or her margins in the same old-fashioned manner—by adding what we call creature feature Ford options and by adding things such as whitewall tires. The more options the dealer added, the less the cars looked like something "European."

We thought we saw an opportunity there. What if we added some more Mercedes-Benz styling cues and partly paid for them by deleting some American options (such as whitewall tires)? Then we'd have a unique product offering—a Mercedes-Benz look-alike at one-third the price of the real thing. [Weren't we violating our selling principles by selling on price? No. We were selling out of category; everybody knew our product wasn't a real Mercedes. Our cars had a certain antistatus cachet—like VW beetles with Rolls-Royce grilles or the Volkswagen Rabbit up against Jaguars and Mustangs and Cougars.] The whitewalls, as I recall, saved us thirty-five dollars per car, which just about paid for the hubcaps we used. We decided to *bet on the come* and do it. I was only a twenty-three-year-old kid at the time, but Dad gave me the job of making it happen.

Eventually I chose to add Mercedes-Benz–type hubcaps and a "250 LM" signature on the trunk lid and also a Mercedes-Benz–type hood ornament. I mounted the radio antenna in a rear fender just like a real

Benz, changed the trunk lock cover over to a Lincoln cover, and pin-striped the bottom of the car. Where did I get the hubcaps, 250 signa-ture, and hood ornament? I went over to the local Mercedes-Benz deal-ership and bought them at the parts window! The Mercedes-Benz hubcaps fit right onto the Monarch rims—they were both fourteen inch. The "LM" part of the signature was meant to stand for "Lincoln-Mercury," and I got that out of the Lincoln-Mercury parts bin. In a very short time, I'd put together our prototype "Mercury-Benz."

The public loved the car! We sold the prototype car and had demand for many more. We menu-priced them at a level that gave us a fair profit, and started selling Mercury-Benz cars by the gross—thirty-five to forty *a month*. Needless to say, I became a pretty regular customer at the Mercedes parts window—until we got a very official-looking letter in the mail from Daimler-Benz telling us to "cease and desist," or they'd sue us. I panicked and ran to Dad, who told me I'd gotten us into the mess, and I'd have to figure a way out. Big help! That's one of the won-derful things Dad did for us kids; when he gave us responsibility, he gave us *total* responsibility. If we got in the soup, we'd have to find our way out. It was his way of telling us he trusted us.

I was caught in a bind. On the one hand, I didn't want to lose those thirty-five to forty sales a month; we were doing very well with the Mercury-Benz. On the other hand, I knew I had to quit my visits to the Mercedes parts window. And in fact, it didn't take Mercedes regional management very long to figure out where I got the parts and then shut me off. They only had to look at their parts orders to see that one dealership was selling far more hubcaps and stars than all the rest put together.

What did I do? Well, with Dad and John Pagano's help, I scrambled around and found a willing hubcap manufacturer in New York and flew there for a meeting. We designed a symbol for the hubcaps—a stylized *T* for "Tasca" that looked much like a Mercedes inverted star. We found a local jewelry manufacturer to make a T hood ornament with a circle surrounding the T just like Mercedes-Benz. The same company made 250 LM signature plates for the rear deck lid. We were back in the Mercury-Benz business in a matter of weeks. That program lasted until Ford discontinued the product line in 1979. Over the four-year period, we sold thousands of custom Mercury-Benzes. I occasionally still see one on the road today.

About a month after we'd gotten back into the Mercury-Benz busi-ness, Dad was out on the new-car lot, and he saw a tall, Germanic-looking guy pull up in a new Mercedes. The guy got out and walked over to our Mercury-Benz section. He didn't notice Dad watching him. He looked our product over very carefully, and then said in a soft, forceful voice: "Goddamn it!" We knew we had them.

MORAL:

Bet on the come.

Selling Performance

The next strategy we hit on involved performance. In the 1960s, people wanted performance; everyone, not just the kids, wanted fast cars. We saw an opportunity there to make a lot of money satisfying our customers. How did we do it? We began to package performance cars by ordering the right components out of the Ford parts bins. Back then, if you knew which parts to order, you could make a hell of a performance car for not very much money; we learned how to do it, and we went around the country in a specially equipped tractor-trailer truck teaching other Ford dealers how to sell performance. To tell our story, we created Team Tasca—the most successful street-class drag racing team ever. Recently, I was inducted into the Drag Racing Hall of Fame for Team Tasca's achievements. Throughout the entire period, our win rate at the track was over 90 percent.

Remember, I don't measure success by money; I measure it by *achievement*, and we achieved a lot in those years. Our story line in effect said: Buy your performance Ford from the same people who make them for Team Tasca. We distilled our sales philosophy into this simple story: *"Win on Sunday, Sell on Monday."* With that story, we outsold everybody in our area in the performance car segment of the market. Lee Iococca ultimately borrowed that story for the entire Ford Motor Company. People still ask us today: "When are you going back into racing?" I tell them, "When we believe we can be number one." I don't want to do anything just to be second.

During that period, we created a number of unique cars to stimulate our regular customers' interest in our performance car offerings. I guess you might say that we created the equivalent of the Detroit Show Car—except that our cars were based mostly on regular production street cars. In 1965, for instance, we won the Milestone National Championship NHRA Drag Racing Winternationals using a factory experimental Mustang. We made that car into the "Tasca 505"—the car that won *American Hot Rodding*'s 1965 Car of the Year Award. That award was presented in front of the Glass House (Ford Headquarters) in Detroit, with Don Frey of Ford looking on. In 1968, we created the Cobra Jet Mustang. Such cars ultimately stimulated sales of the more normal, showroom performance Ford products.

The success of Team Tasca also allowed us to capture a small but lucrative market: We sold more cars to the very high performance set in our market area than anybody else. Our cars all became local legends. In 1969, we topped off our racing success with the Street Boss, the fastest street machine ever. We continued to sell performance content to our customers until the bottom began to drop out of the performance car market in the early 1970s—brought on by the emerging new emissions requirements and then by the oil embargo.

The Street Boss

—Bob Tasca Sr.

In the early 1960s, there was a period in which Chevrolet was really cleaning Ford's clock at the track. I wasn't too pleased about it. A guy named Bill Lawton kept coming around to my dealership and rubbing it in; he drove a 409 Chevy that was winning big, and one day he pushed me just a little too hard. I remember pointing a finger right in his face, and saying to him: "Lawton, you'll never win another race in a Chevrolet!" He laughed, but I think I shook him up a little. I was very serious.

The next day, I started building my first superstock race car, a car based on a 1962 Ford Galaxie two-door. We built that car in three weeks. That next Sunday, we showed up at the Charlestown Raceway with the Team Tasca Galaxie. With our mechanic John Healey driving it, we clocked 13.3 seconds in practice. Lawton's best practice run was 13.6. When Lawton found out I was faster than Chevy, he asked if he could drive the Tasca Ford in the actual race! I said sure. Of course, he won. After his first run, he asked if he could become my permanent driver. Again, I said sure.

Of course, the Chevy dealers hated him for it. But he told them: "The Big Bopper made a statement: You'll never beat Ford in a Chevrolet. Now some of you think he's a big BS-er; but I say, he makes BS happen."

From then on, we owned the top end of the performance car market in our part of the country. Lawton and all of his buddies started buying cars from us. Bill was my driver for the next ten years—right up until we quit racing. He was inducted into the Drag Racing Hall of Fame along with me in June 1995.

Toward the end of our racing decade, I built a car called the Street Boss—the fastest street machine ever. The amazing thing about the Street Boss was that while it won at the track it was a perfectly manageable car on regular roads; I used to drive it to and from work. It got to the point where nobody would race me—even when I wasn't driving the Street Boss or another performance car. I could drive home from work in a Falcon 6 and nobody would race me; they were all so intimidated that they figured I must have a Street Boss engine under the hood. Let me tell you, being known as the "Street Boss" didn't hurt my dealership's performance car sales one bit!

MORAL:

When you make a credible threat, be prepared to back it up.

Blueprinting

When the performance era ended, we began to search for another way to sell hot product at a menu price that would satisfy our customers and give us a fair profit on each customer we made happy. An opportunity had already begun to appear in the American car market. I'd like to tell you we seized on it, but we didn't; we sort of stumbled into it. You see, the quality in American cars had begun to slip in the 1960s, imperceptibly at first, but after a number of years, the cumulative difference began to be obvious. The growing quality slippage offered us a new opportunity, but we didn't see it at first.

Why did quality slip? Well, the makers began to see their costs go up due to the new government regulations. They'd always competed on the basis of cost and didn't know any other way at the time. So, they began to take labor cost out of the product, to make up for the emissions and safety content they had to develop and put in. They took labor cost out the dumb way back then; they sped up the assembly lines. (Now, we take it out the smart way; we *design* it out.) The workers had less time to do each job, so of course, the jobs were done poorly.

That's why Henry Ford II came to me in 1967 and asked me if I'd rebuild a standard Ford for him to drive—he knew it wasn't put together right. Well, we did it, and he loved it. Several years later, he asked me, "Tasca, why don't you start debugging cars for your customers?"

That's what he called it—"debugging." I said to him, "You know, that's a great idea. I ought to try it."

And I did. That's how we got into our next strategy for menu-pricing cars.

By then, the performance car era was dead, and I had switched to Lincoln-Mercury from Ford. Once something no longer sells, I lose interest in it fast. I realized that my new customers had a little more money to spend than my Ford customers, so I began to consider Mr. Ford's comment seriously. I rebuilt a Lincoln to my own demanding specifications, and I advertised it: "Buy Your Debugged Car from Tasca." That was the original story. Well, two things happened. First, my new customers showed immediate interest in what I was offering them. Second, I got a visit from my friendly Ford district manager who came down to cancel my franchise—because I was indicating to the public that Ford Motor Company cars had bugs in them! I said to him, "Well, is that a secret? You mean, you think that Ford Motor Company car owners believe their automobiles are perfect?"

He said, "Well, you can't use the word *debug* then."

I said, "That was the chairman of the board's suggestion—that I use the term *debug*. But, if you want me to change it, fine. I'm not against it; I'll call it something else."

So, I called it "blueprinting." Maybe that was an influence from my racing days, where we blueprinted engines—made them actually conform exactly to their design blueprint. At any rate, the idea was this: Every car, every product for that matter, has a set of blueprints that show how it's to be built. If you actually build it to the blueprint, the car should be perfect—in regard to that blueprint.

Unfortunately, the designs being released by Detroit back then weren't perfect. And when you get a variance of materials and labor going into the car, you get imperfection also. So, what I was doing with blueprinting was rebuilding the car to be as close to the blueprints as possible. Practically from day one in the Lincoln-Mercury store, we offered a blueprinted car program. What was the story that supported the product package? "Drive a car like the chairman's." We didn't say who the "chairman" was; if people asked, we told them either Henry Ford or Bob Tasca. It didn't matter which; people loved the idea. It was real exclusivity.

The Tasca Assembly Plant Visits

—Bob Tasca Jr.

Dad is the guy outside the company that helps make "Quality Is Job 1" at Ford happen inside the assembly plants. When I go with him on some of his Ford assembly plant visits, I'm amazed at how everybody responds to him. There's literally yelling and cheering going on. The workers love him. They know he's tough, but they also know he's on their side. He wants to help them build the best cars in the world. When he goes through a plant, you'd think it was Henry Ford from the response he gets.

Sometimes, I think he starts to believe that he *is* Henry Ford—that he actually owns the Ford Motor Company. He really loves Ford, and he's done an awful lot for the company—and never collected a dime for it. But every once in a while, we have to pull him back into reality and remind him that he's not Henry Ford, he's Bob Tasca.

We charged the customer about 5 percent over our regular menu price for a blueprinted car. We didn't make any money on the blueprinting; depending on the individual car, we lost a little or made a little. We didn't do it to make a profit on the blueprinting service; we did it to guarantee two things: our ability to sell product at a menu price and our ability to gain a repeat buyer. You see, once a person actually experienced owning and driving a perfect car, he or she didn't want to settle for anything else. Our repeat business on blueprinted cars—pretty soon our customers began to call them "Tasca-ized cars"—was amazing, about 98 percent. About 33 percent of our customers chose them. Besides blueprinting, we offered the owners of these cars the most comprehensive service package ever given a customer. We actually offered three levels of car preparation and service back-up, with three different menu price levels. We called it the "ABC Plan," and it is reprinted here just as we presented it to our customers.

The Tasca ABC Plan

Plan A

Your car is completely blueprinted. What's "blueprinting"? It's a complete and thorough preparation of the car by Bob Tasca's group, like the ones the "chairman" prepares for his private use. Tasca refits it as closely as possible to what the factory intends it to be. This includes door fits, window leaks, wind noise, squeaks, rattles, and upholstery neatness, refining and setting up the power train for maximum drivability, vibration free. In short, the "perfect car." After "blueprinting," your car is test driven for approximately 200 miles by Bob Tasca or one of his sons, just to make sure it is "perfect." Your car will come equipped with all-weather steel-belted radial tires. Should your car ever require service, you'll get a loaner at no charge. You'll get a coupon book representing 3 percent of the selling price, which you can use as cash to pay for Tasca service, and coupons good for 30 car washes per year for two years at convenient locations. Unused coupons are redeemable after two years (or sooner, if the unit is traded) toward the purchase of any Tasca car. At the end of the first and second years, except for physical damage, we'll redetail your car to make it look like new again. Our plan should free you from any expense on service or appearance for two years. We do practically everything except chauffeur your car for two years.

Plan B

We'll "blueprint" your new car as per Plan A and give it an in-house wash when you bring it in for service, and you have the use of a loaner at no charge. The price of the car under Plan B is less than under Plan A—naturally.

Plan C

Normal predelivery, plus interior and exterior cleaning. Under Plan C, you get less than under Plans A or B—but you pay less.

The credibility we gained from blueprinting enabled us to sell all our cars on a menu-price program. We wouldn't bargain, and we wouldn't talk price. We had a flat rate price for every car—7 percent over our cost for a standard car, 12 percent for a blueprinted car. Everyone now bought at the same price, so nobody could say he was taken, or that he wasn't given as good a deal as someone else. The only difference was what we would pay for the trade-in.

Blueprinting also made the cars more valuable at trade-in time, because we knew the car was blueprint-perfect at delivery and maintained that way by our service department. So a blueprinted car was actually cheaper to *own*, even though it cost more to *buy*, because it was worth more at the end of two years. So, blueprinting also helped us *shorten our trading cycle*—at a time when people were tending to keep their cars longer. And the customers tended to brag about their blueprinted cars while they owned them, so a lot of people were waiting in line to buy them from us as used vehicles. That way, we got a fair profit on both sales of the same car—new and used.

We continued the blueprinted car program all through the 1970s and into the early 1980s. The program couldn't last, though, because we knew that the domestic makers would either have to improve their quality or go under; either way, we'd eventually have to find another opportunity in the marketplace to base a menu-price strategy on.

Again, I'd like to tell you we were so smart that we hit on another terrific opportunity ourselves, but it just didn't happen that way. You see, *I got to be so successful because I listened to a lot of other people who were smarter than I am*. In this case, it was a man named Eustace Wolfington. Eustace really launched us on our next strategy, and story, for menu-pricing product. This time, the strategy and the story didn't involve making the automotive ingredients hotter in the marketplace; it involved making the product more *afford-*

able to the common person. We didn't change the automotive product directly; we changed how the customer bought the product.

That change constituted nothing less than the "Second
Revolution" in automobile ownership, and I'll tell why in the next
chapter.

10

How to Buy a Car:
The Smart Way and the Dumb Way

Financing: The Second Revolution

The worst investment you can possibly make is to borrow money to purchase a depreciating asset.

—ANONYMOUS

You shall know the truth, and the truth shall set you free.

—JOHN 8:32

Occasionally, one of my new Lincoln customers will say to me, "Bob, I'm seriously thinking about buying a car from you. But frankly, I'm confused. I've been taught that the smart way to buy a new car is to pay cash—and then keep the car for a number of years to make the investment pay off. But your salesman is telling me something different. I just don't understand."

The fact is, these people are partly right in what they've been taught. The worst way to buy a new car today *is* to take out a conventional auto loan. When you do that, you're borrowing money on a depreciating asset. (An automobile really isn't an investment at all; it's a big consumable expense. You buy a car to use it up, to consume it—not to realize a yield from it.) But even in a cash-purchase situation, a car is a big prepaid expense—not an investment at all. As a purchaser, the pertinent question to ask is, How do I minimize my _cost of usership?_

Often, the customers who approach me to express their confusion are older and wealthier—people who haven't yet fully discerned that there's a Second Revolution going on in how we buy cars. You see, Henry Ford created the First Revolution in car ownership: He made it possible for people to _buy on time_. That meant people didn't have to _save_ first and _use_ later—a real burden for most people. The revolution I'm talking about, the Second Revolution, began right here at Tasca Lincoln-Mercury in 1982.

What _is_ the Second Revolution? Rather than buying on time, you _pay as you use_—that is, you pay for the car as you use it up.

Do you know what I say to people who ask me if they shouldn't make a one-lump-sum cash purchase payment? I ask them a question in return: "How do you want to buy a car—_the smart way or the dumb way?_"

Now, I wouldn't recommend _you_ say that to _your_ customers; it could be taken as highly offensive. I get away with it, I guess, because of my age—nearly seventy. I've spent over fifty years building up enough integrity so that I can speak bluntly. But the fact is, the dumb way is to pay cash for the whole car; the smart way is to buy the use of half the car. Here's the true story behind that realization.

Buying Only Half a Car

It all began in 1982 when I got a call from Joe Cappy, the general marketing manager for Lincoln-Mercury Division. He said, "I'm going to send a guy named Eustace Wolfington down to you. He's either the greatest BS-er in the world, or he's a genius. One or the other, but we don't know which."

Now, don't take that as a put-down directed at Ford; several of Ford's managers including Bob Rewey, Lincoln-Mercury general sales manager at the time, had the good sense to listen to Eustace when nobody else would. As it turned out, Rewey had been bouncing his ideas off of Ford managers and dealers for about a year when I got that call. Rewey was asking me to make one of the final judgments on Eustace's ideas, which are presented in the box "Pre-Trade Plan Core Ideas."

Pre-Trade Plan Core Ideas

True Cost to Drive = Selling Price – Resale Value – Repairs

Package new automobiles with content that gives the customer the "best value relationship" between selling price and future resale value with no repairs—the lowest-cost way to drive. Then, customers can actually drive a higher-priced car for less cost than the lower-priced models.

Trading Cycle Management

Choose a trading cycle that returns the customer to the sales door before he has to spend money on repairs and while his car is in greatest demand as a used car: Maximize resale value and minimize repairs.

Shift the Resale Risk

Let the financial institutions assume the resale risks to make it possible for the customer to make a buying decision based on lowest "true cost to drive," rather than on selling price.

Well, after Eustace came down and I listened to him for two or three hours, I made up my mind that Joe Cappy was right—he was either one or the other, and I leaned a little toward the genius side. I decided I could use his ideas for a whole new program—a program that would enable me to sell a lot of cars, and make a lot of people happy. Eustace had the dream of making a *well-equipped* new car affordable *every two years* for the common person; he wanted to give Americans the lowest-cost way to drive a new car. He also dreamed of finding a permanent way to eliminate all the horse trading that goes on in our industry (translation: one-price menu selling). So you see, we shared a dream.

I told Eustace that together we could make his dream become a reality. Then I went to the Ford Motor Company, and I told them

I'd run a test program using Eustace's plan along with my business philosophy. I asked the people at Ford, "If our program works, will you adopt it for the whole Ford Motor Company?"

They said yes. And that's just what has happened. Today, Ford calls it the Red Carpet Lease program. Originally, however, Eustace called it the "Pre-Trade Plan," and I'll tell you why in a moment.

The First Core Idea: True Cost to Drive

Eustace, it turned out, was a man on a mission—a man sent to do nothing less than change the way we think about purchasing automobiles. His first core idea was stunningly simple: If a customer bought a new car only wanting to use *half* of it (in other words, use it for two years and then trade it in on another one), why should he have to finance the purchase of the *whole* car? Why not turn the process around? Instead of paying for the whole car, and then selling it back to the dealer at an uncertain price, why not have the customer pay for only the half he intended to use—with the option to buy the other half in two years at a known price if he chose? Obviously, it would cost the customer far less if he had to pay only for the half that he used. And it turns out that that's just about how much you use up in two years—one-half of the original price.

Let's talk a little more about this half-a-car idea, because I think the concept, and the Pre-Trade Plan generally, also has implications for businesses that aren't car related.

Supposing a customer were given the option of financing only half of a new car's total value and only for two years? What would happen? Well, it turns out that the monthly payment would be about the same as a conventional four-year car loan. In other words, the customer could *drive new every two*—and for about the same cost as he'd previously paid to buy a new car every four years. Now that should open your eyes. In fact, that became one of our stories we used to sell cars on the Pre-Trade Plan: "Renew Every Two." We also used "While your neighbor's changing tires, you're changing cars." Those are pretty powerful stories. We've sold a lot of cars, and made a lot of people happy, using just those two stories.

If the "renew every two" concept is such a great idea, you may ask why nobody thought of it before Eustace. Well, the answer turns out to be simple. The workability of the idea depended on the dealer's ability to gauge the value of the used car two years out. You see, you couldn't very well have the customer pay for what he'd be using up in two years unless you knew ahead of time what the car would be worth in two years. And predicting future resale value was considered a stumbling block.

Before this time everybody believed that every used car was different—that predicting the future value of cars was for psychics only. The bankers all believed it. That's why they would only loan money on the purchase price—not on the amount you were going to use up. Eustace, however, had studied the used car auction market long term, and he'd discovered something stunningly simple: on the average, a two-year-old used car tended to be worth wholesale one-half of what it listed for new. He also discovered that every individual make and model had its own resale value percentage—some exactly 50 percent, some a little more, some a little less. But they all averaged out to one-half, year after year after year. What that meant was that you *could* predict the future value of each car with various equipment options two years out at the time you sold the car new.

What Eustace had done was to apply the Lombardi principle for winning at football to the car business. The Lombardi principle advocates breaking a "game" down to its smallest components, and then estimating the outcome percentages for each. For a dealer—or customer—playing the auto finance game, the components were selling price, resale value, and *true cost to drive new*, and Eustace found that the critical *true cost to drive new* percentage tended to be *half the car.*

What is the true cost to drive new? It equals the selling price less the resale value, but only for a new car held for no longer than two years. Why two years? After that, another variable enters into the true cost to drive equation—repairs.

By the time I met him, Eustace had convinced a number of banks to accept his financing concept, but he realized that he needed a car manufacturer to package the cars and help make the entire concept work. Ford was the only car company that had listened to him.

Are there other industries where you can apply the Lombardi principle? Of course. The obvious example is the insurance industry, but take the securities arbitrage business as another example. There, the idea is to make investments in merger and acquisition *situations* rather than in stock *portfolios*. You break each situation down into its component pieces and estimate the probabilities for the outcomes; then you bet on the come—take a position in the merger or acquisition situation, being careful to hedge your bets. You can make a lot of money in arbitrage with very low risk, but you first have to totally change your thinking about investing.

The Second Core Idea: Trading Cycle Management

What does the Pre-Trade Plan offer for each of the players in the new game—finance companies, car companies, dealers, and customers? For each, it beneficially *shortens the trading cycle*. Customers trade every two years—not every four to six—thereby ensuring a repair-free lifestyle for a cost that is the same or even less. And the finance companies, car companies, and dealers all do more business.

You see, what had been happening since the 1950s was that as cars became more expensive (due to added creature features and then government-mandated antipollution and safety gear) the average length of the loan period had been stretched out to make payments more affordable. By the early 1980s, it was up to as much as five years.

The following table shows what was happening. The nature of the loan instrument—the same monthly payment over the entire loan period—meant that the customer paid mostly interest and little principle, until near the end of the loan. In effect, the long-term auto loan instrument put the customer upside down for most of the four- or five-year loan period. The customer couldn't afford to trade more often, even if he wanted to: He owed far more on the car than it was worth in the used-car market.

Decade	Average Loan Period (months)	Average Trade Cycle (months)	Average Loyalty (percent)
1950s	24	26	60+
1960s	36	41	40
1970s	42	45	29
1980s	48	52	25

This table clearly shows what had been happening to customer loyalty percentages as the average loan period stretched out—they'd gone in the tank. When people stopped buying new every two, their loyalty plummeted precipitously. Falling customer loyalty concerned the car companies greatly. That's why Bob Rewey at Ford listened to Eustace in the first place—Eustace promised Rewey that he could do something about the situation. Even at Tasca Lincoln-Mercury, in spite of our blueprinting program, our customers' average trading cycle had gone out to seventy-seven months by 1982, and as I've pointed out before, absence doesn't make the heart grow fonder.

The Third Core Idea: The Most Able Should Bear the Risk

Let's go back to the story of how all this got tested at the Tasca dealership. When Eustace and I started running the test market Pre-Trade Plan for Ford later in 1982, we were the only two people in my dealership to believe in it. Even my sons didn't believe in the beginning. Fortunately, some key people at Ford also believed in what we were doing, and they helped make it happen. At first, it was very tough. What we were trying to do was change people's whole way of *thinking* about how to buy an automobile. We were asking them to buy the *use* of the car for two years, *half the car*, with an option to actually buy the car itself, *the whole car*, at the end of two years if they wanted. They weren't taking title to the whole car right up front, with a finance company lien on it, like they were used to doing. So you see, we had to change their *beliefs* about ownership—and that wasn't easy.

For each customer, we'd present the comparative numbers—two-year lease versus a four-year loan—and then show each person how they could actually *save* money on the Pre-Trade Plan. We also explained that they were gaining *two options*. One was the *priceless option* that we offered them no matter how they bought from us: the Tasca family commitment—You *Will* Be Satisfied. The other was the *priced-out option:* They could know when they bought a car *exactly* what the car would be worth in two years. Ford Credit and the Ford product divisions assumed the risk on what the car would actually be worth; the customer no longer had to.

In two years, our customers could exercise their options: They could either complete the purchase of the car (at the price we gave them when they bought it—"the residual value"), turn in the keys and walk away, or turn in the car and take another new one. If they chose to buy out the whole car in two years, they paid no more than if they'd bought the car outright in the first place. Wouldn't you buy a car with such an option—especially if it didn't cost you anything?

Over time, the difference between "renew every two" and "borrow every four; own for five" really added up for our customers.

There was a lot of worry for the first two years under the plan over how our customers were going to exercise that priced-out option. Nobody knew for sure. Obviously, both Tasca and Ford hoped they'd exercise their options to take another new car—that was the whole point of the program for us. Ford was curious to know how many Pre-Trade customers would take another new car at option time—proof positive of increased customer loyalty. Ford Credit was worried that all the chickens would come home to roost at its doorstep—that as management they'd be stuck with cars that turned out to be worth less than the residual values, and that nobody would want to buy them at the residual. Then, Ford Credit would take a bath on the cars. I was worried that I might for some reason have unsatisfied customers, and Eustace was worried that his whole dream might slip away.

Let me tell you what happened. Eustace had told Ford that 60 percent of the people we sold on the Pre-Trade Plan would renew under the plan—that is, turn in the car and take another new one. Now, that would indicate tremendous customer loyalty to Ford products. At that time, remember, customer loyalty was shrinking throughout the auto industry; Ford's was only about a third of 60 percent. Well, when the customers started coming in to exercise their options, it turned out that Eustace had been wrong. In fact, he was _way_ off. They didn't renew at 60 percent; they renewed at 80 percent!

What a wonderful way to be wrong! That kind of customer loyalty was simply unheard of. Today at Tasca Lincoln-Mercury, we have more than a thousand customers who've renewed every two years for the past ten to fourteen years. That's how I define customer loyalty. How would you define it?

The Easiest Sale in the World

—A customer

I got a call a little while back from my salesman at Tasca. He reminded me that even though I still had three months to go on my lease, I was getting a little high on miles. I said I knew that, and it was beginning to worry me a little. He said he thought he had the answer; how would I like a new car identical to the one I was then driving—for less money per month? At first, I was astonished. It was about thirty dollars less than I was now paying to drive a nearly two-year-old automobile. Then I said to myself: "What the heck! I like the product; I don't have any reason to change models." So, I said yes. Three or four days later, I drove over to the dealership, and they swapped my plates. I drove off in a brand new Mercury Marquis—for less money. Was I pleased? You bet.

I learned later that the salesman had my car presold to a used-car customer before he even called me. I guess the guy wanted a Champaign Marquis, and mine was the first used one due in. I hope the guy likes the car as much as I did.

Right after the renewals started, our car sales simply took off. Until 1984, as I've already mentioned, Tasca Lincoln-Mercury's trading cycle with its customers was way out at seventy-seven months—our customers traded for a new car with us every 6½ years. We were selling only around fourteen hundred new cars a year, and we were working very hard to make those sales—few of them were repeat purchasers. By 1986—the first year we made number one in Lincoln-Mercury sales—we'd climbed to more than thirty-six hundred new cars. The reason why isn't hard to see. Each year starting in 1984, on top of our new customers, at least 40 percent (one-half of 80 percent) of our two-year Pre-Trade customers renewed and took another new car. It wasn't too long before one-half of all our new car sales were renewals—remember, a satisfied customer is the easiest one to sell. And a Pre-Trade customer is the easiest customer in the world to satisfy: She never has the car long enough to become unhappy with it. By 1994, ten years after we sold our first renewal cars under the Plan, our average trading cycle had come down from seventy-seven months to twenty-nine months. Are we satisfied? No, not until we get it down under twenty-four months.

Thinking about the Pre-Trade Plan

The Pre-Trade Plan succeeded in test market beyond our wildest dreams. It was spectacular! When we started showing 80 percent repeat purchase rates, Ford management really sat up and noticed. They kept their commitment to Eustace and me and made it possible for any Ford Motor Company dealer to sell cars under the plan. Today, Ford does nearly a quarter of its new car sales as Red Carpet Leases—and all the leases are only out two years. That's all Ford Credit writes. Ford leases more of its cars than any other auto company. The other companies all favor leases with longer terms—three years or even more, and they lease less.

You might wonder why. In what follows let me try to cut through some of the confusion about leasing.

First of all, you need to understand that the Pre-Trade Plan *is not primarily about leasing* at all—that's a smoke screen put out by journalists. It's about the *lowest-cost way to drive new.* It just happens that in America due to various government regulations, the lease is the best financial instrument to use to allow people to renew every two with no resale loss risk to themselves. In a way it's unfortunate that Ford chose to call the Pre-Trade Plan the Red Carpet Lease—because that confuses people. We sell the lowest cost way to drive a new car.

When the leasing term goes from two years to three years, it's now a financing strategy that's being used—not a lowest-cost drivership strategy.

Why? As I've already told you, after two years, repairs start to enter into the equation, and costs go up—including the psychic cost of *worry* (Will my car break down? Will it be tied up in the shop for repairs? etc.). While we at Tasca sell the lowest-cost way to *drive new* through pretrading, the other car companies' dealers sell an alternative financial arrangement that offers the customer the chance to pay more to drive an older car.

If you're still not sure which route is preferable, take a moment to think about the *hidden risks* to car ownership. What about the loss in resale value caused by an accident or a manufacturer's recall? A car that's been in an accident, for example, is often permanently worth less—even when it's expertly repaired. A suspected manufacturer's defect, if it's widely publicized, could permanently tarnish the reputation of a model, even when necessary changes have been made. The plan helps protect you from all that.

After all, risk should be borne by the economic agents best able to handle (read: *insure* against) it, and that's the finance companies and auto manufacturers, *not the customers or the dealers.* So you see, the current revolution in auto ownership isn't really about leasing; it's first about customer risk reduction. Wouldn't you like the *freedom from worry* that pretrading offers?

I haven't even mentioned the biggest single *hidden cost* of automobile ownership: *tyranny of price.* Think back to the "Six Hundred Strippers" story. Remember, nobody wants a stripper—a car without the desirable creature features. But occasionally, a customer will grit his teeth and buy one, either because the *price* for the well-equipped alternative is too high, or he can't afford the loan payments. Unfortunately, he gets hit with the double whammy that the car has low resale value. So not only does he have to drive a new car he hates, he also had to pay a huge hidden cost—the value difference at trade-in time between the stripper and the well-equipped car. That's the *tyranny of price.*

Under the Pre-Trade Plan, the average customer is freed from price tyranny. Because we can predict the future value of cars with different content—different levels of equipment—we can order in prepackaged products equipped for the highest resale value. We then show the customer how *he can drive a higher-priced car for lower cost!* In doing so, we eliminate the *unnecessary cost* of driving. The table "The Hidden Cost of Driving" demonstrates this.

The Hidden Cost of Driving: An Example from 1982

Component	A Stripper	A Well-Equipped Car
Selling Price	$9,000	$10,000
Resale Value (in two years)	$4,000	$6,000
Cost to Drive	$5,000	$4,000

Give away the Risks; Share the Gains

Do you know what else we do for our new car customers under the plan? If their cars turn out to be worth more wholesale than the residuals as "useful cars," we give them the difference! We give them the gain! When they take special care of their cars, we reward them. On the other hand, if the residual was set too optimistically, that's the leasing company's problem. The customer doesn't have to pay. In other words, under the plan you as our customer get the best of both worlds. If your car's value should happen to go down to less than the residual, you're protected. You don't have to pay. If your car's value should happen to go up over the residual, you get the gain. Either way, you win.

Now think about it. Under the old way to buy a car, the conventional loan, you frequently would lose either way. If the car's resale value went down for some reason, you owned it, and you took the loss. If it went up, you might still not get the gain, unless you had good market information when you went out to horse-trade for another new car. The Second Revolution in car ownership has changed the results of the game from lose-lose to win-win for the customer. The next time you go out to "buy" a car, don't *buy* it at all. Pay only for what you use, and convert your personal automobile game from lose-lose to win-win. I promise you, You *Will* Be Satisfied.

Trade Cycles Revisited

Clearly, as a customer you win big time under the plan. Don't, however, overlook an incredible benefit to a business person using the plan. Not only is the trading cycle shortened but the uncertainty over *when* the customer will trade is practically eliminated. Remember, the uncertainty of when, not *if*, a customer will trade again bedevils every big-ticket-item business. One solution is to try to work the "Lonely Maytag Repairman" sort of a strategy, hoping that if you do enough reminder advertising your customer won't forget you at trade-in time. The other solution, the preferred one, is to *eliminate the uncertainty*. That's what the plan does. It enables me as a businessman to know right down to the month when it is that the customer I sold an expensive product to today will come back to me for another one. She *has* to come back in two years—

even if it's just to return the car. It's up to me and my co-workers to make sure that when she does, she takes another new one along with her. When you find a way to manage your trade cycle, rather than let it manage you, *the future is now.*

How Can This Help Me in My Business?

Unfortunately, the pretrade business concept applies directly to few industries right now. The retail automobile industry is rare in that it has an efficient used-product auction market. That means that resale values for used product can be easily predicted. It also means that as a dealer I have almost instant liquidity for the used product I handle. That means that the Pre-Trade Plan can work in the auto business more efficiently than it can almost anywhere else. In most other industries, you as the dealer have to make your own market in used product, and that's more costly than when you have a ready-made market available to you.

But you can still make a version of the Pre-Trade Plan work for you if you're in an industry such as expensive jewelry, RV's, private aircraft, yachts, condominiums, or high-quality appliances—to name just a few. To make it work, though, you have to pay the costs of creating a used-product market. If you can pull it off, the payoffs are potentially huge. Ultimately, it's a test of your own resolve.

Let me close this discussion of the plan's applicability with one simple example. The Electrolux company makes and markets high-quality vacuum cleaners, among other products. It also reconditions and resells its older products taken in on trade. Other companies, of course, do the same thing. The reconditioning program isn't just a little side business; it helps *validate* in the marketplace the high prices Electrolux gets for its new machines. By creating value in its used products, Electrolux makes a number of things happen, all at once: It satisfies those customers who want an Electrolux but who either can't or won't pay the price for a new one. It enables the company to charge more for its new products; clearly, they'll fetch substantially higher prices than the used products, particularly if they contain exciting new content. And it reduces the cost to buy new—because the customer can be shown how much her older machine will be worth on a trade.

Could Electrolux make the full conversion to selling on usage cost, not on purchase price? I don't know for sure. I do know that if company managers could successfully market the idea, they could reduce their customers' trading cycle length immensely. They could also conceivably make their future so certain that they could base much of their production planning on their present sales—in so many time periods, so many customers who bought in this time period will come in to trade for a new machine! They'd make a lot more people happy and make a lot of money doing it.

I believe there's a lot of everyday opportunity for making markets in what I call "useful" products—products that may be used to me but that could be new to you. For instance, many Americans like new clothing on a regular basis—long before the old has worn out. The new-to-you market in clothing, however, is presently not very efficient, and it's pretty thin. I found that out firsthand when I tried to get rid of about twenty-five business suits I'd accumulated!

Here's an idea: If you presently run a dry cleaners and/or Laundromat business, why not think about making a market in new-to-you clothing for your dry cleaning customers? You'll lower their clothing costs and create new customers for your business— the ones who'll love your new-to-you clothing offerings.

Is there a similar challenge awaiting you in your business? *Think about it.*

11

Even the Undertakers Wouldn't Buy: Predicting the Hot and the Not So Hot

Even the Undertakers Wouldn't Buy: A Lesson

A few years back in our industry, we saw a period in which many automotive interiors appeared as various shades of gray. In the Ford Motor Company, we were offering about eight interior colors—and half of them were gray! Imagine it—four different shades of gray! Why did that happen?

Well, first of all, gray was the legacy of an earlier era when available technology didn't permit car makers to market cloth upholstery resistant to stains and dirt. In the 1930s and 1940s, most car interiors were drab and dominated by gray. But in the 1950s the auto companies began moving away from cloth upholstery; vinyl became the material of choice because it could be cleaned and kids couldn't destroy it. The plus was that color choice exploded. The minus was that we all sat on vinyl seats that were cold in the winter and clammy in the summer.

Things began changing again in the 1970s, and it became possible to make cloth fabrics that wouldn't stain or soil easily. The technology came from America, but the Europeans led the way in replacing uncomfortable vinyl with the soft feel and pleasant colors of wool and synthetic blends. When the car companies in

America finally responded, they got the technology right, but the aesthetics wrong. You see, the executives making the color choice decisions were older men with engineering backgrounds. They naturally chose cloth combinations of gray, believing they wouldn't show dirt and stains. Somehow, they overlooked the fact that the stain problem didn't exist anymore with Scotchgard-treated fabrics.

(Incidentally, a Scotchgard treatment is one of those backdoor ways to reclaim profit that many of today's auto dealers offer; at Tasca we refuse to sell it, because the materials used are *already* protected against staining. *Further* protection is unnecessary.)

The executives also chose gray because that was the color that had been recently selling in vinyl and leather. They made the fatally flawed decision to offer what *had* been selling, rather than what *would sell.*

So there we were at the Tasca dealership with four shades of gray—colors so lifeless *even the undertakers wouldn't buy.* We were stuck with them because we had the wrong sort of people making those decisions. For years, I pressed the Ford Motor Company to have women make the color choice decisions—especially for vehicle interiors. I suppose there are those out there who'll disagree, but it's always seemed to me that women are more naturally attuned to the subtleties of color. Anyway, an important breakthrough came when we marketed a small pickup truck called the Splash.

The Splash's interior design challenged the common wisdom that truck interiors had to be utilitarian. The Splash was sensuous; the colors were stunning. I'd encouraged a young Ford industrial designer named Bonnie Cunningham to really pull out all the color stops for that product, and I was gratified to see the product really take off.

Since then, Ford's gotten women much more involved in the design of its interiors, especially in the choices of colors and materials. And the results show; the company's product interiors have become warm and exciting. The undertakers don't fancy the new color schemes either, of course. They're now too lively rather than too dead! But I think we've made giant strides. The point is that when it comes to product you need to be able to judge between the quick and the dead.

Doing Nothing Is Worse Than Nothing:
Betting on the Come Revisited

Choosing gray for four interior color combinations gives you an example of what not to do with product decisions. Whether you're a product maker, or a product retailer, when you make a color decision—or any other decision that affects what the customer can *see, feel, or touch*—you're counting on a certain market direction. You're betting on the come, whether you like it or not. As I've pointed out earlier in this book, you can't avoid the bet by treading water. As opposed to hanging back from the action in a gambling casino, the refusal to place a bet in the marketplace still constitutes a bet—and the worst possible bet at that.

Let me illustrate with an example. We all know about clothing product lines that bomb in the marketplace; the department and specialty stores run sweeping sales to clear them out. In such cases, the buyer bet on the come and lost. Does that mean the buyer would have been better off not to have placed a bet on the future direction of the marketplace? Not at all: Quite frequently in the clothing business, nothing is *more* dead than last season's best-seller.

This reminder that for a business person there's no way to avoid risks may discourage you. But remember, risk can be reduced. Over time, developing the ability to judge between the quick and the dead allows you to bet on the come with efficiency.

The Cycles Beneath the Chaos

To many business people, the market appears to be whimsical at best, perverse at the worst. Predicting what will sell takes on the nature of a crapshoot. Customer preferences seem to have no clear pattern. The whole process seems chaotic. The truth is, it's much more orderly than you think. Underneath the chaos, not only are there patterns for behavior but most markets show fairly regular cyclical happenings. Not only that, the cyclical happenings in *some other industry's marketplace* may be leading indicators for your own industry. By that, I mean *signposts pointing toward the future* direction. If you can read the signposts correctly, you'll find your way through what otherwise appears to be a chaos of product offerings.

This goes far beyond what the economists try to predict with *their* leading indicators—which is the level of future economic activity. As a business person, you can use the signposts for the future to predict not only the future sales strength of your market but also future product preferences within your marketplace, that is, what exactly your customers will want in the future.

Recognizing the signposts allows you to change the odds in your favor when you as a retailer or wholesaler order in inventory— or when, as a maker, you make design and production decisions. Betting on the come no longer means betting your company on a whim; it now means pursuing the *least risky* future course for your business.

The automobile industry has, in fact, over the years served as a signpost for a number of other industries—home appliances manu- facturing, for instance. When autos became glitzed up with chrome, what happened to home appliances? The appliance manufacturers put on chrome, too. On the other hand, automobile styling itself has used boats, locomotives, and aircraft (remember, the WWII P- 38 fighter provided the inspiration for the finned era in auto design) for styling direction. In each case, one industry provided another with a signpost leading to successful future product innovation.

Signposts for the Future

Let me give you a real example of how we at Tasca use certain sign- posts in our business. I watch two industries very closely—women's clothing and home furnishings—because I know that their cyclical trends are strong indicators of how the auto industry will move, albeit with a lag built in. For instance, women's hemlines move up and down in a cyclical manner. When hemlines start moving up, two things happen in my industry: General sales interest on the part of consumers increases, and more important, interest shifts from more conservative to more sporty automotive products. When hemlines move up, you don't want to get caught with a car lot stocked with conservative sedans. Of course, the opposite also holds: When hemlines start down, unload your sporty product quickly and get into more conservative product offerings. Does this apply only to your female customers? No. It holds for the purchase habits of men as well.

The clothing colors that women choose signal two additional things: They indicate the direction a dealer should move regarding the choice of automotive colors, and in a more general way, they indicate the strength of the consumer market. Muted, as opposed to strong, colors indicate that auto color choices will soften. They also point to conservative buying habits.

Together, women's clothing hemlines and color choices indicate the future strength of the market and the direction that both model choice and color choice will take. I order my inventory accordingly, and most of the time I guess correctly.

The home furnishings industry also indicates future automobile preferences. Here, the dealer can read the signposts for a longer cycle as well as get another reading on color preferences. The styles of home furnishings fluctuate between formal and casual—on a significantly longer cycle than women's clothing preference changes. Interest shifts as well between inside and outside the home.

For instance, the two current strong interests in the present automotive marketplace—minivans and sport utility vehicles—surfaced first in the mid-1970s and then in the early 1980s. And in each case, the trend was presaged by changes in home furnishings and home lifestyles. In fact, sometimes the signal was there before the products had even been conceived or reached production.

Let's talk a bit more about the minivan craze, which, ironically, had its origins at Ford.

I knew that a product taking shape in Hal Sperlich's mind and on his drawing board at Ford in the early 1970s would be a winner. Sperlich was a great car man and a real design genius. Right from the beginning, Sperlich and I brainstormed that minivan product and worked to develop it. We both knew that there would be a future need for such a product: We could *read the signposts*. In Ford circles, the product even came to be known as the "Bobcat"—short for the names of two of my sons—Bob Junior and Carl A. Tasca (CAT). I did everything I possibly could to sell Henry Ford II and the board on that concept, but their caution got the better of them and they turned it down.

Remember, that was the late 1970s, and things were looking pretty grim in Detroit. Ford had already bet big on a method to meet federal fuel efficiency mandates; they weren't too excited about what seemed like another huge roll of the dice. They decided to pursue some safer bets.

What happened? After Henry fired Lee Iaccoca, Lee went over to Chrysler. Hal Sperlich had already joined Chrysler by that point, and he hadn't given up his dream of putting the Bobcat into production. Well, Lee figured he had nothing to lose, so he bet on the come and adopted the minivan concept as his own. He knew—from looking at the signposts—that if he could ever get that product into production it would be a runaway sales success.

And, in fact, he was right. The product that Sperlich's team put together at Ford became the Chrysler minivan, and it went on to dominate the market.

The 3 Percent Principle

If I ordered in only the product that suited me personally, I'd sell about 3 percent of the market.

—Bob Tasca Sr.

I believe that many business people order in product in a way that actually *increases* their chances of failure. They fall into the ego trap; they come to believe that *what they like, their customers will like, too.* Or, in the case of some automotive executives, they come to believe that choosing how cars will look is a privilege of leadership, a reward for having successfully climbed the corporate ladder. It's a bad mistake, because more often than not those ego-driven products fail in the marketplace.

Look what happened to General Motors in the late 1980s and early 1990s. The company launched billions of dollars of new product offerings—literally dozens of new models—and nearly every one of them failed. GM executives ignored the most fundamental principle of leadership—that leadership is not a reward but, rather, a constant challenge for the future—and they lost.

Do some business people succeed in running ego-centered businesses—in selling lots of product they like? Yes, a few do, in markets where the customers are as ego centered as the shop owners. But remember, it's only a few.

I know for a fact that if I ordered in only the product that I liked, I'd sell about 3 percent of the market. That's all. So I never do it. When I order in product, I always remember that I'm representing my customers. I need to watch out for their interests. There is only one area of my business where I follow my likes, not those of most of my customers—and that's in the area of quality. I'm a quality fanatic. When we deliver a car to a customer, it must be as close to perfect as we can possibly make it.

Now, I know that only about 3 percent of my customers will consciously recognize all the differences in quality we insist on. But here's the thing: The 3 percent who *will* notice tend to be the most vocal of my customers; if I let them down, they're likely to tell other people, and my reputation will suffer. So we consciously aim to please the 3 percent to make sure that the other 97 percent never have cause to doubt they're getting the best.

The Real Cost of Cold Product

There's yet another thing many business people do that actually *increases* their chances of failure: Once they've ordered in the wrong product, they hang on to it. They suddenly put on their accountant's hat and fall in love with counting it and making sure it's there. It's the business person's analog to something I call *librarian's syndrome*—the desire on the part of some librarians to have every book in the library, on the shelf, in its right place. If you want to take a book out or even take it off the shelf and look at it, they glare at you. They forget that books are meant to be read. Similarly, many business people seem to forget that product is meant to be sold—not inventoried.

What is the real cost of cold product—product that just sits on the shelf? It's not the cost of the product itself, although that may be heavy enough. No, *the real cost of cold product is the cost of the sales you lost because of the money you have tied up in it*—the cost of the many people not satisfied because *you* let the product just sit there. The real cost of cold product is what economists call its *opportunity cost*, the cost of your failure to take advantage of other opportunities in the marketplace.

When I order in the initial product for a selling season, I order in one of every color. Then I conduct a little experiment: Which colors sell quickest? Usually they're the colors that my market signposts *tell* me will sell. But, by ordering in one of each color, I get a quick check on the market. Based on the experiment, I narrow down the colors I order in bulk to about five. What's the rule? If a color sells in thirty days, we reorder it; if it doesn't, we get rid of it and never reorder it again.

What do I do with the ones that don't sell? They constitute cold product, and I unload them as fast as I can. I absolutely hate cold product. You should also. Don't play Miriam the librarian.

Rules for Finding Hot Product

- **The product commitment rule:** Never commit to last season's product; always read your market's signposts.
- **The colors rule:** When it comes to such decisions as colors and textures, women seem to know better (sorry guys!); if you're a business*man,* watch what women like, not what you like.
- **The cycle principle:** Markets are never chaotic; look for the regular cycles and the orderliness of markets underneath the seeming randomness.
- **The real cost of cold product:** The cost is equal to the sales you lose because you hang on to it; don't play Miriam the librarian—treat cold product like the plague: Get rid of it.
- **The stock/build rule:** Always build or order what you believe your customers will want in the future.
- **The leadership principle:** Leadership is not a reward for what you've done in the past so never treat it that way; leadership is a constant challenge regarding what you can do in the future.
- **The 3 percent rules:** If you order in or build what *you* personally like, you'll sell about 3 percent of the market; always maintain the strictest quality in everything you do and sell—only about 3 percent of your customers will notice, but if you fail them, they may tell the 97 percent who wouldn't otherwise have noticed.

12

Quality Is Job 1:
The Story behind a Revolution

Why It Can Be Good to Swim Upstream

I knew that in order to satisfy my customers, I had to influence the product.

—BOB TASCA SR.

As a Ford dealer I realized early on that to satisfy my customers I'd have to achieve some measure of control over the product I sold. That's part of the reason why I've stayed loyal to Ford for more than fifty years: When you become opportunistic with your suppliers, you lose all chance of influencing their behavior. I know that most of my fellow dealers—in fact, most retailers for that matter—just take the product they get as a given; that's what they have to sell, period. Or they change suppliers or add suppliers to their product offerings: They become opportunists. Either way, they give up all chances of influencing their supplier(s). The last thing they think of doing is working upstream with their suppliers to benefit their customers.

Looking at my own industry, I'm amazed at how few dealers take advantage of the opportunities they have to influence automotive product. When I run my dealership seminars, I often ask participants what they're doing about a product problem I know we all have. They just shrug—as though it's not their job to represent their customers with the factory.

Part of the reason some dealers don't get involved with improving the products they sell is pure selfishness. Why should I give the factory my time, they say, when the result is going to benefit my _competitors_ too? Well, I've never worried about who else I might benefit, so long as I help my customers.

Let me give you an example. From day one, I'd been involved in the new redesign of the Taurus-Sable automobiles that entered the market in the fall of 1995. For five years, I'd busted the butts of Ford managers, engineers, and designers to make sure that car came out right. I _haunted_ them. The designers and engineers gave me nearly everything I wanted in those cars. Why? Because Ford executives know I'm speaking for my customers.

At a key juncture, the company sent two prototype 1996 Tauruses down to my Ford dealership for us to go over. We found several things the factory people had apparently missed, including a right rear door that I couldn't make fit the opening exactly. Now don't get me wrong; the factory people really _care_ about product, and they've found literally thousands of glitches and have corrected them. The point I'm making is this: If you're a retailer, the manufacturers really _need_ your input as a customer representative—to help them get the product right, and right the first time around. It costs far more to redesign the product _after_ you've started to build it, then it does to get it right the first time.

Well, in this case, the factory people measured the door with a micrometer and found that what I said was true—the prototype metal stamping for the door hadn't been made to specifications. They fixed that and some other things we found as well before the first production car started down the line. You see, one of the reasons why the Tasca organization has gained a certain amount of influence with the Ford Motor Company is this: We don't just complain about something that's wrong; we complain and _then_ we show them how to fix it.

I personally spent two and a half days going over those automobiles; I gauged every opening, right to the mil. Most of my fellow dealers would probably think I'm crazy giving Ford that much of my time. I don't. *I'll do practically anything to benefit my customers.*

The days are long passed when it was acceptable for a maker—any manufacturer, not just the car companies—to introduce a new product with poor quality, and then gradually work the bugs out as production cranked up. Customers will not accept that; I certainly won't let my customers accept it. When the new Taurus-Sables started down the line in the fall of 1995, they were absolutely right—and from job 1. Let me tell you about how big a change that actually represents.

Quality Is Job 1: A Story

You may recall the Ford Motor Company's catch-phrase "Quality Is Job 1" and wonder where it came from. Well, *job 1* in auto company lingo is the first production car of a new model to go down an assembly line. Traditionally, the quality that went into job 1 was absolutely *dreadful*—nobody on the line knew how to build the car yet. The companies didn't devote time to preproduction training; they just set up the line and started it; the workers learned how to build the car by doing it. Obviously, just about the last car you'd ever want to own was a job 1. The cars got better with practice, but they still left a lot to be desired—even at the end of a several-year model run. That remained the situation in 1980. In that year, you may recall, I was still blueprinting cars for my customers.

In 1980, when we blueprinted a Lincoln Towncar for a customer, my co-workers and I put in an average of seventy hours to make that car right. (Today, my crew needs about twenty minutes to do the same job—just enough time to make sure everything's right; that's how far we've come since 1980. Just look at the quality of a Towncar today; it's stunning.) I knew that something had to be done, and at the level of the factory. The factory couldn't go on expecting its dealers to fix what was wrong with the cars; too many of the dealers just wouldn't take the time, and it was terribly cost-inefficient.

So, I went to see Red Poling in the summer of 1980. At the time, Red was Ford's executive vice president. I told him I wasn't sure I could continue as a Ford Motor Company dealer; product quality was just too awful. It was a credible threat, I guess—credible because I ran one of the most successful dealerships in the country. Red looked alarmed, and he asked me what I would do about the poor quality if I had the opportunity.

I said I'd start at the top plant—the Wixom plant where we built Lincolns and Thunderbirds—and I'd convene a group of people from all areas of the Ford Motor Company, including assembly line workers. Together, we'd determine how to boost quality immediately. After all, if you can't do it in the plant where you build your supposedly highest-quality cars, where can you do it? Then, we'd go on to start fixing the other plants.

Notice, I didn't say: "Give me two billion dollars and I'll show you what to do." That was the General Motors way of doing things, and I knew it would never work. I knew that Ford didn't have that kind of money, and I knew that money wouldn't fix the problems anyhow.

Remember, at that time things were getting bleaker by the week for Ford; the company was on a negative roll that would run up losses exceeding two billion dollars over the next several years. So much was wrong with the company that I don't think Red Poling or anybody else even knew where to begin to fix it all. I told Red he had to start with *quality*—that if we fixed quality, everything else would fall into line.

On the other hand, if we didn't fix it, nothing else anyone did to improve the situation would matter. I knew that if the company made public commitments to quality, it would be like giving the public a *hostage:* We'd have to deliver on quality. We'd be held accountable.

What happened next, I regard as my most significant accomplishment in a lifetime spent working with the Ford Motor Company. In August 1980, I got together with Red Poling, Bill Scollard, and about two thousand Ford employees—all at the Wixom assembly plant. The people who attended included plant managers, engineers, designers, product-planning people, and plant workers. From that meeting emerged an unprecedented commitment.

The Wixom Commitment was a pledge by Red Poling on behalf of the Ford Motor Company that we would in the future build best-in-class cars, measured on a world standard, and have the world know it. It was a statement of purpose that turned the company completely around.

I give Red a lot of credit for making that decision. In doing so, he started a process that today allows every Ford employee and Ford dealer to say that Ford builds the best cars in class in the world. After that day, Red never once said no on quality. Over the years, he authorized literally billions to make the commitment happen. You might say that Red made a big bet on the come—he bet that our vastly improved quality would earn the company big profits, and it has. What's more, that commitment has permeated the entire company, creating a sense of pride that is without parallel in the auto industry.

Although Red started the commitment, when Don Petersen became president and then chairman, the whole character of the company changed under his leadership. Don understood the importance of the workers' commitment to the quality process. He became the chief architect of Ford's amazing gain in people's respect. No one did more to change the personality of the Ford Motor Company than Don Petersen did with his corporate mission statements.

Anyway, what happened right after the Wixom Commitment was amazing. Ford shut down the entire Wixom plant for three weeks, so that the most glaring problems with the plant itself, identified in our meetings, could be fixed. I don't know what it cost, but it was a daring thing to do at a time when the company was hemorrhaging cash very badly. When the plant started again, quality soared; the assembly line workers believed that things would change—and so they did.

Today, the new chairman, Alex Trotman, has the same commitment to quality. Alex will not walk away from quality. If I called Alex up right now and said, "There is something wrong with your product and I want to correct it," he'd say: "Carte blanche—do it." I know that. It's not just lip service. Ford is dedicated to being the number one quality producer in the world.

I knew after the Wixom Commitment that Ford would need a simple story to capture what we were about to do. The story line I urged the company to adopt was ultimately encapsulated in the slogan "Quality Is Job 1." Every industry insider knew what *job 1* stood for at the time—a terrible automobile. By using those words, we were saying, "We're going to transform the whole meaning of *job 1* at Ford."

Of course, back then the story line was meant more for Ford workers than for Ford customers. It became something that thousands of Ford people would live with every working day of their lives—just as my co-workers live with "You *Will* Be Satisfied."

Over a ten-year period, the results exceeded our expectations. I watched 3.5 quality-level cars go to the 8.5 level, and that's one hell of an improvement (car quality is graded on a 10-point scale; 10 is perfect). Today, an 8.5-level car is the *minimum* acceptable level in the company. We *will* eventually build 10-level cars at the Ford Motor Company; some are already there. We have the design and technical capability; we have the people talent. And, yes, we've made the capital investments, although we've never just thrown money at a quality problem. Do you know what it really takes to do it? *Wanting to do it.*

After we began the "Quality Is Job 1" movement at Ford, Red Poling asked me if I'd help with the overall direction of the quality program in the assembly plants. I said sure. Now, this might strike you as a little strange. "Tasca," you're saying, "you mean to tell me you're an overseer of quality at Ford—and you don't even work for the company?" That's right. I didn't *want* to work for the company; Red would have gladly hired me, and I could have made a lot of money, but I wanted to stay where I was, doing what I was doing. I assured him I could still oversee Ford assembly plant quality, worldwide, and I have.

Everything I've contributed has been based on my knowledge of two things: first, motivation, honed by the motivation programs Vince Lombardi and I used to run for Ford, and second, the technical aspects of the products. Remember, I started out as a mechanic (and a pretty darned good one, too), and I spent more than twenty years blueprinting Ford cars to make them right. People used to call me "the gauger" because I walked around with a body gauge to measure every fit. Ironically, of the two knowledge areas, probably the most important has been the motivational, not the technical: Ford Motor Company people have to *want to make it happen*. But I also realized that I had to know the product better than anyone else to be a reliable judge of how good, or poor, quality was in each plant.

What I did ultimately was to create a quality award—the Tasca Award for Excellence—to be bestowed on individual assembly plants. I had a lapel pin made up as a symbol for excellence, and the only way the people in the plant could receive it was if the plant attained a certain specified level of quality. The award continues to be bestowed today, and the Ford plants compete like hell to get it. If this reminds you of Team Tasca, our dealership service brotherhood, don't be surprised. It should; it's much the same concept, carried out on a far larger scale. At first, we couldn't set the standards too high, or nobody would win. We started at a 5.5-level car and have worked up from there. Today, the minimum is 8.5, and a number of our plants are building 9-level or better products.

Once the award was publicized, I began to make assembly plant tours, checking on quality. Over the years, I've traveled over a million miles and made hundreds of plant inspections for Ford, worldwide. My role has been to set standards and incentives; the Ford workers have done the rest—and I'm very proud of them.

You see, to get the award, a plant has to *prove* to me that their quality is at or above the standard. I go there, and I pick the cars that I'll measure for quality—they don't. That way, nobody can cheat by salting away particularly good cars for me to check. There is only one way to get the Tasca Award—and it's by producing quality. That's why the award is so coveted: You can't buy it or cheat to get it. You have to get it the old-fashioned way, by earning it.

Do you know what my personal goal is for 1996? I want to see every Ford assembly plant receive the award. And it can happen. We're that close. Why do our production people strive to be number one in quality? It's not for money, although I'm sure that Ford rewards its winning assembly plant people. It's for *recognition*—for the knowledge that they're the best in the world at what they do.

How Do You Read an Automobile?

You can't make a silk purse out of a sow's ear.

—OLD APHORISM

Quality is a term that has developed a certain mystique. People *think* they know what it means, but individual definitions vary. Let's make it simple from an automotive perspective. I once told a senior vice president at Ford that I could read the quality of an automobile just by looking at the front of the car. He was flabbergasted. "How can you do that," he demanded.

I took him out into the parking lot at Ford headquarters, and I showed him.

Here's how it's done. I start at the left front corner of the car, and I sight down the tops of the left-hand doors, checking to see if they're even. If they're even at the tops, the rest of the door fits pretty much have to be right. Then I judge the evenness of the gaps around the hood opening, and I check the tops of the right hand doors. Without even looking at the rest of the car, I now have a pretty good idea of the quality level of the whole car. Why? I know that if a plant's workers took the care to get this much right, the rest of the car can't be too bad. You can do the same thing; it's easy— once you know how to read a car. Of course, to read a car in total detail, I also need to check the fit of the trunk lid, and all exterior trim, and then check the fits for all interior components. Thoroughly evaluating a car's quality level is fairly involved.

Am I *just* concerned with fit and finish? No, but, as it turns out, the fit-and-finish quality dimension is all you can hold an assembly plant accountable for; the rest of a car's quality derives from either design and engineering or from the components and subassembly makers. Fit and finish is what I call short-term quality, and I'll explain that in a moment.

The quality level on a scale of 1 to 10 that a car reads out at is merely a representation of the fit-and-finish standard present in it. And it's only partly under the control of the assembly plant people. The fact is, the short-term quality level is determined by two things: design and assembly accuracy. For instance, if a car has been designed to a 3.5 quality level standard, there's no way on earth that an assembly plant can build an 8-level car from that design. It can't be done. What an assembly plant *can* do, if its people are very good and very motivated, is boost the quality level of that car from 3.5 to perhaps 5.5. They can never make it into an 8-level product, though. To build an 8- to 10-level car, you've got to start with a

design at least pretty near a 10. That's why we were building only 5-
to 6.5-level cars back in the mid–1980s: They hadn't been designed
any better than that; in fact, they'd been designed to be worse. Our
workers actually made them better than they were.

Test Scores in the Sixties

—Bob Tasca Sr.

Back in the 1970s, I once gave a lecture to a large group of Ford engineers in which I asked them this set of questions: "How many of you
graduated from engineering school with examination test scores in the
sixties?" It's not surprising that nobody raised his or her hand.

"In the seventies?" Still, nobody raised his or her hand.

"In the eighties?" Some people raised their hands.

"I have to conclude," I said, "that most of you got eighties and
nineties in engineering school." They all nodded in agreement. Clearly,
they were pretty proud of their engineering expertise.

Then I asked them another question: "Well, if you all got eighties
and nineties in school, why are you willing to sign off here on designs
that are only worth sixty points?" Silence reigned. Nobody said a thing.
"I have to conclude that you were motivated to do quality work in
school, but you're not motivated here. That's got to change."

MORAL:

In whatever you do in life, aim for a ten. You still may not make it,
but you'll certainly fall short if you're willing to sign off on a six.

Never disparage American workers; look for the *institutionalized*
reasons why product doesn't live up to expectations. We couldn't do
any better in the assembly plants, not because American workers
didn't care or weren't skilled enough, but because company leadership hadn't motivated its designers to do better. It had proven the
old adage: If you see your company as a dog, it will become one.
Today, the Ford Motor Company is still a dog—but it's a world
championship show dog. Why? Management's attitude changed. I
give people like Don Petersen a lot of credit for that.

At the Ford Motor Company, we began to design 8-level cars in the early 1980s, but because of the long design-to-production cycle time back then, they didn't appear until some six years afterward. We began to design 10-level cars in the late 1980s, and now our customers are seeing the real fruits of the Wixom Commitment: Ford builds best-in-class cars worldwide and lets the world know it.

The Twelfth Commandment

Don't cheat on your customer—where she can either see, feel, or hear it.

—BOB TASCA SR.

I just told you that fit and finish constitutes short-term quality. Clearly, there must be something called long-term quality as well, and together, they must add up to total product quality. Short-term quality is what the customer is able to read from the product in your showroom. I call it "short term" because it lasts *in the customer's mind* only until she drives off the lot in her new car—or leaves your store with any new product. Mostly, short-term quality consists of fit and finish; fit and finish constitute *signposts* for the customer. The customer believes that if the fit and finish look good, the car probably will treat her well. The reason why I've devoted so much of my life to helping Ford achieve best-in-class fit and finish is simple: Short-term quality helps me sell automobiles.

I also care, though, about what I call long-term quality. Most of what constitutes long-term quality is called "NVH" in the auto business. *NVH* means "noise, vibration, and harshness"—what the customer can either hear or feel. The assembly plant can't do very much about NVH—except to fit to a level that eliminates some leaks and wind noise. NVH must be designed out of the driveline and platform application.

But why is that important? Well, long-term quality begins to matter to the customer the moment she drives out of the dealership. If long-term quality hasn't been designed and then built into the product, she'll come to hate it.

I care about long-term quality because it determines to a large degree my customer's loyalty to me. If I sell her a car that develops annoying habits when she drives it—things she feels and hears—

she'll dislike that car more every time she drives it. If she notices that aspects of the car are visibly deteriorating—things such as paint work or trim work or upholstery—it will bother her more every time she looks at it. No matter how good my service people treat her, she'll never be satisfied. How likely will she then be to come back to me for another product?

Out of my understanding of quality *from the customer's perspective*, I've formulated another customer satisfaction business principle so fundamental that I call it the Twelfth Commandment: *Don't cheat on your customer—where she can either see, hear, or feel it.*

Notice, unlike other commandments for customer satisfaction, this commandment can get kept only by the product's *maker*; when the maker breaks it, the product's seller gets hurt along with the product's *taker*—but the seller has no control over it. The Twelfth Commandment provides the maker's *Customer Satisfaction Road Map* from the inception of a product's design right through to the product's delivery to the retailer. Pay attention to what it says: Don't cheat on your customer in any area of your product where she is likely to *detect* it. The Twelfth Commandment applies to every maker of any product, not just to automobile companies.

You may be asking: Does this mean it's all right to cheat on your customers in other areas of the product? Yes, it does. Because, you see, there's only one way a maker can cheat on its customers without them knowing it in the long run—and that's by taking out product content *and cost* that the customer doesn't care about in the first place. When you eliminate cost that benefits nobody, you actually improve the product by making the product more affordable in the long run for the customer.

I personally know of only one maker—and it happens to be an automobile company—that has flagrantly broken the Twelfth Commandment and still lived to tell about it: Rolls-Royce. The people at Rolls-Royce for many years now have very conscientiously loaded their product with costly content that nobody can see, hear, or feel. But of course, they don't build cars; they build monuments.

The Moving Goal Line

Why has Rolls-Royce built cars with undetectable content—at least until recently? The answer is simple: The definition of quality changed, and the company's management and workers didn't. They continued to design and build cars to the quality definition and standards of medieval craftsmen. Think about it. What did quality mean to people as recently as the 1930s and 1940s? It referred to the *materials* that went into the product and how well materials were crafted together.

Do materials still define quality today? Not the way they did then. Today, you can't have the *absence* of high-quality materials. The American car companies discovered that when they tried to continue using upholstery material that cost seventeen dollars less a yard than the material the Japanese were using. Resale value for American cars versus Japanese cars plummeted in the late 1970s and early 1980s—partly, at least, because some materials we used were cheap. There's no magic to high resale value; unless you use high-quality materials, you're not even in the running. Today, everybody uses them.

The customer's definition of quality changed by the 1970s to include fit and finish—partly because people had become disgusted with how makers were cheating on the visible part of quality and partly because technology began to offer new quality horizons. *What can be accomplished will be, and people will adjust their product quality expectations to what has become possible.*

Automobiles and many other products could now be built to technical standards never before imagined. Soon, the definition also expanded to include reliability—because new technology offered the promise of a greatly enlarged reliability envelop over time. Notice what has happened here; the location of quality has now expanded to reside not only in the product itself, but also in what the product *does.* Products can be designed and built to be much more reliable for much longer than ever before. Quality now also includes the dealership's services to the customer. What's the underlying principle here? In any product class, q*uality is a moving goal line.*

Quality is a moving goal line on two dimensions. First, the very definition of what constitutes quality *in the mind of the consumer* changes over time. Second, the level of the actual quality delivered on that definition increases over time. For instance, on the fit-and-finish quality definition, the standard has gone from around 3.5 to

8.5 over the past fifteen years. Will it continue to go up? Probably not much, and for two reasons. First, people do not buy absolute quality—they buy quality offered at a price. As the standard goes up, generally speaking so does the cost. Second, the definition of quality itself will probably change—to include another cutting-edge dimension that assumes greater importance.

Today, for most products quality is still fit and finish and reliability. What might it become tomorrow? Perhaps "environmental friendliness"—the recyclability of the product. Why might this happen? Well, partly because materials, fit and finish, and reliability have nearly become nonissues: Most brands of most products have these quality attributes to fairly high standards—or they won't sell. Also, as technology makes recycled products possible, they'll be more in demand.

What's the lesson in all of this for the average business person? Just because you deliver the best quality—or for that matter, satisfactory quality—today, don't assume that it will be the best or even satisfactory tomorrow. Quality is a moving goal line. Delivering the best quality is a constant challenge. You can't satisfy your customer unless your quality standards continually change and improve. *The best never rest*.

Quality and Content—and Value

Sometimes people confuse quality and content. They're not the same thing. Content resides in the product; it includes those things that define the class of product. Obviously, a clothes washer has to wash clothes—and do so reliably. But the product also includes the critical elements that I call creature features—the additional content the maker designs and builds in that enhances the value of the product to the customer. Quality is *how well* the maker designs in and builds in the content decisions.

So, obviously, you can have extremes such as the bare bones product built to very high quality—a VW Beetle, for example—or the luxury product with lots of features that are always failing. The Twelfth Commandment says that, whatever content level you choose, you must deliver quality that your customer can *sense*.

Quality and content must never be pursued *for their own sakes*. When either or both become goals for their own sakes, *cost* to the customer goes up—and to an unacceptable level. That's what happened to a number of Japanese companies, including but not limited to the auto companies. When you pursue additional content (creature features) and additional quality without regard to cost, you find that two things happen simultaneously: The marginal additional cost to you the maker for either goes up explosively while the value to the customer hardly goes up at all. _Value_ here means additional content and/or quality that can be sensed, divided by additional cost—all to the customer.

Pretty soon what happens under the absolute pursuit of quality and/or additional content is that the cost can't be passed on to the customer. The marketplace forces the maker either back into reality or down the road to bankruptcy. For product makers, as well as product retailers, a high road of excellence leading to leadership into receivership does exist—and it consists of the absolute pursuit of content and/or quality.

As a simple example, consider the case of the Japanese auto companies and their pursuit of closer tolerance panel fits. When the Japanese redefined fit quality as a consistent 4-mil gap between body panels, everybody cheered; customers loved it, and now that's become the de facto industry standard. But when some Japanese companies pursued a tighter standard, they found that their production costs exploded, while the customers couldn't tell the difference. As a result, the standard has stayed at 4 mils.

Is that all there is to quality and content? Not quite. Quality and content can be seen to exist in the product itself, but they have to get communicated to the customer. Otherwise, _they have no value._ How can a maker communicate value and content? The maker needs to create a story. The story can then be told directly through advertising and public relations, or the story can be told indirectly through wholesalers and retailers. Of course, wholesalers or retailers may also create stories of their own—which add to the value of the maker's story and actually create new value for the customer. Any way it gets made or communicated, the story must be simple in order to be memorable, and it must _create additional value_ for the customer.

What does that additional value consist of? It consists of a compelling reason to buy the product. For example, when we created the "Life Saver Sable" story, we extended the product's safety-related optional content into a simple but powerful story: This product can save *your* life. That was so compelling a reason for people to buy that they willingly paid more than a thousand dollars extra for it. When product makers attempt to convert their dealers/retailers into merely service centers, they lose among other things the powerful potential for these businesses to create a compelling story.

Can content and quality get created only by makers? Of course not. Increasingly, competitive content and quality are coming to include how the customer is treated by the seller throughout her trading cycle. The goal is becoming customer *loyalty*, and that's replacing sales as *the* goal for any business. That's what the customer satisfaction revolution is all about—extending content and quality concepts to include how the customer gets treated, all in order to create customers for life. In this sense, *every* business is a product maker needing to "build" product to suit the taker.

Suiting the Taker, not the Maker

Do you know what went wrong in many American manufacturing companies—not just the auto companies—from the 1950s through the 1970s? They starting making product that was designed and built to suit management—not the customer. Specifically, they began to take out cost, and therefore content, that would hurt their customers in the long run. They didn't concentrate on taking out only the content that people didn't care about—something called *value engineering*—they took out content people could *sense*. They figured that if they did it gradually enough, nobody would notice. In other words, they *built the product to suit the maker, not the taker.*

Why did they do it? They adopted the gross profit business agenda; they became dominated by the new generation of finance whiz kids, and they began to set the wrong kind of corporate goals. They remembered their shareholders and, in the process, forgot their customers who also hold a stake in their companies' futures. They began to substitute the old goals set in terms of *sales* for new goals defined in terms of *profits*.

They got away with it for so long because the post–World War II market situation was a highly artificial one; foreign competitors had been pretty much knocked out by the war. Once that situation got corrected, the marketplace resumed its usual role of teacher and discipline officer. Then they suffered until they learned the truth: *You can't make money by saying how much you'll make.* That's circular logic. You *can* make money in the short run by saying how much you will *sell*—and then going out and making it happen. But when you face real competition, even that approach only lasts for a short while. In the long run, you can only make money if you *satisfy your customers.*

I learned that back when I was a grease monkey, and it's just as true today. It's true no matter where your business is located in your industry's value chain. For all product makers, customer satisfaction begins with how you see your product: You must *make your product suit the taker, not the maker.* What's the role for retailers and whole-salers in all this? You must help keep your makers *honest,* and you must make additional overall product content and quality yourself. That's how the Twelfth Commandment applies to you. Otherwise, you're failing to represent your customers; you're letting your customers down.

Find Someone Who'll Listen to You

Serendipity is the facility of making happy chance discoveries.

—Horace Walpole

You may be saying at this point, "All this is fine for you, Tasca. You've got incredible influence with the Ford Motor Company. I can't influence my suppliers' products like that." Well, you're forgetting one thing: I wasn't born with a silver influence spoon in my mouth; I had to *earn* influence—starting from scratch. Let me tell you how I did it.

First of all, I didn't wait until I had my own business to run before I began. In fact, I couldn't have obtained my own Ford deal-ership if I hadn't started influencing the company while I worked for someone else's dealership. This should be good news for anyone reading this book: *You don't have to own a business to begin influencing your suppliers.* In fact, influencing your suppliers as an employee in someone else's business is a good way to start your own business. That's what I did; I earned a Ford franchise at a very young age precisely because I influenced Ford district and regional management when I worked for someone else.

Ford offered me a franchise because regional sales management knew I could add value to the maker's product by how I treated customers and how I cared about delivering product in perfect condition. They liked what I was doing, and I think they learned some things from me about how to treat customers. That's how I began.

After that, two events shaped my future ability to influence the Ford Motor Company's products. One I've already told you the story about—how I went out of my way to satisfy a customer one hot early fall Saturday afternoon and how that customer turned out to be the chairman of the Ford Motor Company. I haven't told you all that happened after that incident, however. When I went to the annual dealer convention in New York City later that year, Ernie Breech made a point of looking me up, and he took me over and introduced me to Henry Ford II. Mr. Ford asked me what I thought of the Edsel car project, and I told him the truth: "Mr. Ford, that car is going to fail." And I told him why it would fail—that the company presently had too many problems with its basic product to succeed against General Motors in an up-market segment. He told me I was wrong.

When it became apparent that I was right, Henry began to ask my views on a whole range of company issues; he knew I wouldn't play company politics with him and tell him what he wanted to hear. We had a close relationship after that for many years, right up until the time of his death. Through Henry Ford, I came to know all of the senior executives at Ford; today, I'm close to the new head of the company, Alex Trotman.

Through all this time, I've never taken a penny from the Ford Motor Company. When the company gave me a brand new Mark VIII for my fiftieth "wedding" anniversary with Ford, I insisted on paying them for the car. Why? It preserved my *independence*. It kept me from feeling obligated and not telling management the truth as I see it.

Notice what sort of event got me in a place to know Henry

Ford. You might call it a fluke or a lucky break; I don't. I call it a _serendipitous_ happening. What's the difference? Well, a serendipitous happening is a happy event that appears to occur just by chance, though some people seem to have a facility for making such events happen. How did I make it happen? I did what I always did for people in trouble—even when they're not my customers and it's inconvenient for me—I went way out of my way for a guy I figured I'd never see again. By consistently doing so, _I made it inevitable that something like what happened would happen._ In a sense, I made my own serendipitous happening.

How? Well, if I hadn't gone out of my way to help out customers, Ernie Breech could have come to my dealership, and I could have turned him away. Most people would have missed the opportunity of a lifetime that way. Also, by consistently satisfying all customers who came to me, it only became a matter of time until I would impress someone like Ernie Breech. It had to happen, and I made it happen. The only thing in question was the details. This is simply an application of the _making it happen principle_, of betting on the come. Anyone in any business can make it happen, can create his or her own serendipitous events.

The second event that shaped my future in the automobile business occurred one year later in Springfield, Massachusetts. At the ripe old age of thirty-one, I participated along with three other guys in a regional dealership seminar presentation attended by a number of much older men in which I caught the attention of Charlie Beecham. Charlie Beecham was one of the last of the old breed of cigar-chomping auto company sales managers; he was also a hell of a bright guy, who rose to be marketing vice president for the Ford Motor Company. After the seminar, he told me he liked how I handled the seminar, and he asked me if I would do a seminar in New York. Now, the New York dealers back then were a tough bunch to work with; not only were they all very opinionated and constantly arguing among themselves, but by now it was 1958 and the market was terrible. That was the year they were all losing money, and that made them even more difficult. It was also the year that Ford lost hundreds of millions, while my dealership made four hundred eighty-nine thousand dollars. So you see, I can say that I've made more money than the Ford Motor Company.

Check Your Hat Size

—Bob Tasca Sr.

After that first New York seminar, Charlie Beecham took me out and bought me a hat. That was back in the days when all men still wore hats. He bought me an expensive Knox hat—twenty dollars. It was his way of saying that I had come of age—that I was no longer a "kid." Three years later, I repeated the seminar, and Charlie took me out and bought me another Knox hat. Then he asked me, "What's the size?" and "What was the size last time?" They were the same. "I'm happy to see they're the same size," he said. That's the point that he wanted me to see; I hadn't let my initial success give me a swelled head.

Do you know what I do today to avoid getting a head too big for the rest of me? The last thing at night, I go out and walk the dogs and then shovel up the you-know-what. That helps keep me humble.

When I got to the seminar, a company man was busy arranging the seating to try to minimize the friction between individual dealers. I told him to seat them all alphabetically and, despite the dire warnings, I made it work.

What did I do? I began by asking them what troubled them. Notice, I didn't begin by *telling* them what they should be doing. We got it all out onto the blackboard; and when we did, we found that we all shared the same three basic problems—poor sales, poor profits, and difficulty retaining employees. I spent the next three hours showing them how to solve their three basic problems. The meeting was a resounding success. After that, Charlie Beecham had me do more dealership seminars. And do you know what? After nearly forty years, I'm still doing them. I eventually began teaching as well at the Ford Marketing Institute in New Jersey. I learned an awful lot about the business by teaching about it.

As a result of the Ernie Breech and Charlie Beecham encounters, I found people within the Ford Motor Company who would listen to me—because they knew I spoke for my customers. The lesson here? In order to influence the product, *you have to find someone who'll listen to you.* To do that, you need to create your own event that gives you a willing listener. Serendipity matters; you can create your own serendipitous events.

Don't Just Complain

The Tasca dealership not only gives you what needs to be done, many times they'll tell you what the problem is and how to fix it. We've had people there [at Tasca Lincoln-Mercury] from every one of our plants, to watch them do predelivery, to learn from them, and then to bring it back and continue it within our process. The Tasca staff has been extremely helpful in that regard, and specific. They don't just complain; they complain, and they offer a solution.

—LOUIS R. ROSS, VICE CHAIRMAN
AND CHIEF TECHNICAL OFFICER OF
THE FORD MOTOR COMPANY

When you find someone within your supplier's company who'll listen to you, don't just complain. Complainers never achieve any influence. People won't welcome you; in fact, they'll hate to see you coming. They'll hate to hear your voice on the telephone. When you find someone who'll listen to you, you need to do two things: Complain about a product problem and then tell the person who's listening *how to fix it*. Being able to fix a product problem depends on two things: listening to your customers and taking a problem-solving attitude toward your business life.

Think about it. Who defines a product problem? You don't; your customers do. Remember, if a customer tells you she's got a problem, she's got a problem. There should never be a question about that. The whole process depends on your willingness to recognize a problem. If you tell your customer that her problem is actually "normal," what happens? You lose the opportunity to solve the problem—and to satisfy her.

On the other hand, if you choose to recognize a product problem, and you complain *and* show your supplier how to fix it, you have the chance to create the serendipitous event that may change your whole business life. You're now on your way to achieving real influence over product, and who knows where it will lead.

You need to decide how you want to go through life: dismissing problems as normal or fixing them. How you choose to look at a problem will define, in large part, how successful you become.

Rules for Customer Satisfaction through Quality

- **To satisfy your customers, you must influence your supplier.** When your customers have a product problem, it's your job 1 to represent your customers with your supplier. Otherwise, how will anything change?

- **To influence your supplier, find someone who'll listen to you.** If you pursue excellence in customer satisfaction, you'll create your own serendipitous events, which will give you someone in your supplier's business who'll listen to you.

- **Never just complain;** complain—and show your supplier how to fix the problem. Everybody hates complainers, but people will respect you if you provide a solution.

- **Quality is a moving goal line.** The quality products or services that you supplied to your customer last year won't be good enough this year. Accept this and start running the race.

- **About 90 percent of achieving high quality is wanting to.** You can't buy it or acquire it through a corporate takeover. Attitude is everything.

- **Remember the Twelfth Commandment:** Don't cheat on your customer where she can either see, hear, or feel it. Cheating where she can't sense it is okay—because then you're taking out content and cost she doesn't care about in the first place.

- **Willingly give your customers hostages for your future business behavior.** By giving a hostage—for example, committing to the slogan "You *Will* Be Satisfied"—you'll keep yourself honest and make a lot of people happy.

- **The New Job 1 Is Customer Satisfaction.** Unlike "Quality Is Job 1," the new job 1 applies to everybody in business: No matter what, satisfy your customers.

PART III

Leading a Customer-Satisfaction Business

13

Listen to People Who Are Smarter than You Are

People and Success

The reason I'm so successful is that I listened to a lot of people who were smarter than me.

—BOB TASCA SR.

Most business leaders are deathly afraid of hiring people who are smarter than they are. It's not hard to understand why: Hiring people who are smarter or who *know more* than they do threatens their control as well as their basic sense of security. There's always the fear of being supplanted.

This fear exists in a more generalized form as well, manifesting itself as an unwillingness even to *listen* to people who appear smarter. The tendency is to dismiss these people as cranks, and that can destroy your chances for long-term business success. I can state unequivocally that a major reason for my success is that I've always made a practice of listening to people who are a whole lot smarter than I am. I've not only listened to them, but I've hired them.

Eustace Wolfington offers just one example of a person I knew I could learn a lot from. If I hadn't listened to Eustace back in 1980,

I'd be nowhere near as successful as I am today. As it turned out, his ideas were pure genius, and I made sure he personally profited from them. I took to heart one of my own rules: *The best way to treat someone who's brought you a great idea is to help him or her make a lot of money from it.*

Let's consider for a moment what happens if you refuse to listen to or hire people who are either smarter or more knowledgeable than you: *You have to do all the thinking yourself!* You have to make all the decisions. That's a terrible burden. Actually, it's worse than a burden; it's a formula for disaster. Why? Well, do you think for a moment that you're smarter than your competitors? If your competitor is not afraid to hire people smarter than he is, and you *are* afraid, who's got more brain power—and who's going to make better decisions?

When you have the opportunity to do so, always hire people smarter or more knowledgeable than you, and pay them well.

As I've said before, the surest way for you to make a lot of money in any business is to help your co-workers make a lot of money. That doesn't mean *giving* them a lot of money, which inevitably leads to favoritism. It means giving them an opportunity to *earn* a lot—by satisfying your customers. Then, you can make a lot, too.

Ordinary People, Extraordinary Results: Creating Ability

Over the years, many of my co-workers have earned a lot of money. I love it when I can help them grow wealthy. Have they all been smarter or more knowledgeable than me? No. Some have, but most have not. Let's consider the matter of ability a little more. Undoubtedly some people are born with greater capabilities than others; it's a matter of genetics. Fortunately, that doesn't have a lot to do with success. Over the years, I've found that *attitude* matters a lot more than simply being smart. I just love people who try hard— even if sometimes they fail. Because I know they'll eventually succeed.

You hear a lot today about genetics and intelligence. If you stop and think about it, it's mostly about the extremes. I'm not interested in the extremes. I'm interesting in normal people with normal intelligence. What factor is most important in the ability of a co-worker to excel? I believe it's the willingness to try. That's what I look for when I hire entry-level technicians and salespeople, for instance. My business practices can *create* superior performance out of very ordinary people—so long as the right *attitude* is there. I can't easily change someone else's attitude. That derives from character—something that's fixed at an early age.

How do we at Tasca create superior performance? We give all of our co-workers the same goal (satisfy the customer), measure each co-worker's performance against that goal, and provide appropriate pay and recognition incentives. As I've mentioned several times, no one at Tasca gets paid on a gross profit; nobody gets recognized for anything other than being best in customer satisfaction.

When we do this, I believe we actually *create ability*. I'm convinced of that because sometimes we hire people who clearly are not the best-qualified people for our sort of work. Or sometimes, they come to us with certain disadvantages that cause other businesses not to hire them. Ironically, these same people often become our best co-workers—because they have a willing spirit.

Let me give you an example of the sort of co-worker I mean: me. I didn't start out life exactly favored. My mother died when I was just a few months old; I was raised by grandparents and aunts. You know how the school yearbooks always identify the students most likely to succeed? Well, I wasn't one of them. I didn't have the opportunity to go to college. For that matter, "the fat mechanic out back" wasn't exactly a compliment. I had to struggle against a lot of disadvantages. I had to work harder than anyone else around me; I still do today.

But I had one advantage denied most of my peers: My grandparents who raised me insisted on instilling key virtues—honesty almost to a fault, discipline, and obedience. When I brought home my report card, my grandfather always focused on my grades in discipline and obedience. He told me I didn't need to be an A student academically to get A's in those categories. Thanks to those *enabling virtues*, I became one of the youngest dealers in the Ford dealership network. Perhaps the reason I can spot people who have an apparent disadvantage but who'll make great employees is that I was one myself. I do that for my own business, and I do it for the Ford Motor Company.

Creating a Business Where No One Has to Lie

So far, I've told you something about the kind of people you should hire if you wish to run a successful business based in customer satisfaction. That leaves the other side of the coin: How do you create satisfaction for your workers (thereby improving the chances of their satisfying your customers)? Well, all I can tell you is what has worked for me: *Creating a business where no one has to lie.*

Let me explain what I mean. A gross profit business sets up a situation in which everybody feels they *have to* lie—both employees and customers. The employees, for example, are told by management that they have to create gross profits rather than satisfied customers. So, they find themselves lying to customers about what's normal for product performance, product suitability or—in an industrial business—delivery commitments. Awareness of this *modus operandi* causes customers to create their own lies—all in an effort to receive the treatment they wouldn't get if they told the truth. Pretty soon, you have a business situation in which everything is based on lies and mistrust.

Because I want to run a business where *nobody* has to lie, I begin with a business agenda and a pay plan that removes the temptation for my co-workers to stretch the truth. My people are told they must satisfy the customer; they receive no bonuses unless they do. Further, they watch me and see that I never lie to the people who walk through the door. So, if there's no incentive for lying to a customer and no behavioral role model for it, it's highly unlikely anybody will do it.

The Twenty-Thousand-Mile Tire with a Nail in It

—Bob Tasca Sr.

Not too long ago, a customer came to me and demanded I give her a new Michelin tire for her Lincoln Continental. She told me the tire had failed after twenty thousand miles—because we'd delivered her new car to her with a large nail in the tire.

Now, I knew, and I'm sure she knew, that a tire wasn't going to run for twenty thousand miles with a big nail in it, and then suddenly fail and go flat. It picked up a nail somewhere in her travels, and it went flat pretty fast right after that. That's what really happened, and she wanted us to pay for the tire so she didn't have to.

You can see that this wasn't really a product problem at all. The tire wasn't defective; it simply met with a road hazard that it couldn't cope with. It was a *people* problem. This woman had paid a lot of money for that car, and she didn't feel it was fair that she should have to pay more now. Further, she'd learned through experience that that's how you get a business to satisfy you—make up a lie and complain loudly enough.

Do you know what I did? I told her she didn't have to worry—that I knew how she felt and that we'd satisfy her. We'd give her the new tire, no charge. I told her, too, that we would have done it for her, even if she hadn't lied. I think she was a little shocked at first. Then, she began to understand what I was saying—that we run a business where nobody has to lie to get what they want. You can tell the truth and still get satisfied. At Tasca, there's no penalty for telling the truth.

It's a fundamental principle: You can't run a customer satisfaction business based on anything but integrity and truth. Why? Well, if something goes wrong, to satisfy the customer you have to fix it. Unless you can learn the truth, you'll never be able to do it. In this case, lies get directly in the way of satisfying the customer.

A Short Course in Human Relations

In many businesses, employees have to worry that if they make a mistake, they'll be fired—the "if you screw up, you're history" attitude. I believe that if you want to run a business based on *truth* and on individual initiative in satisfying the customer, you can't engage in such practices; you can't practice intimidation.

At the Tasca dealerships, the *six most important words* in human relations are *I admit I made a mistake*. At Tasca, about the only thing that can get you fired is *lying*. I tell my co-workers, if you make a mistake, admit it. Tell us about it, and together we'll work it out so that the result will be better than if you hadn't made the mistake in the first place. As I've mentioned previously in this book, that's called failing forward. (It's also called serendipity.) But, never, never *lie* to me.

Do you know what the *five most important words* in human relations are? *You did a good job.* That's the recognition principle. It's a powerful incentive for achieving customer satisfaction. Of course, the corollary to the five most important words is just as crucial: Never tell someone he did a good job unless he *earned* the recognition by satisfying the customer. Everything must always refer back to that.

The *four most important words* are *What is your opinion?* Unless you learn to ask this question of everyone in your business, you'll never be able to take advantage of their knowledge and intelligence. Then, as I've already told you, your competitors who practice the opposite policy will eat you alive.

The *three most important words* are *If you please.*

The *two most important words* are closely related: *Thank you.*

The *single most important word?* *We.*

You'll never achieve excellence in customer satisfaction unless you work as a *team* to satisfy the customer.

What's the *least important word* in human relations? The "vertical pronoun"—*I.*

A Short Course in Human Relations

The Six Most Important Words: "I admit I made a mistake."

The Five Most Important Words: "You did a good job."

The Four Most Important Words: "What is your opinion?"

The Three Most Important Words: "If you please."

The Two Most Important Words: "Thank you."

The One Most Important Word: "We."

The Least Important Word: "I."

People Principles

- Never be afraid to listen to or hire people who are smarter than you.
- If the top management of a business doesn't commit to customer

satisfaction, the middle management will never make it happen. To show commitment, top management must participate in the change process.

- To become successful, help your co-workers become wealthy.
- Successful businesses are built on the extraordinary achievements of ordinary people. Hire hard workers and support and encourage them, even if they fail at first.
- Be willing to hire people who have a "disadvantage." Often, such people are determined to make the most of the opportunity, and the results show.
- Run a business where nobody has to lie. Only by knowing the truth can you solve problems.
- Teach the "Short Course in Human Relations" to your co-workers.

14

Supercharged! Keys to Increasing Efficiency

The Second Way to Make a Lot of Money

As I've already told you, there are only two ways for a business person to make a lot of money. This rule holds whether you run a small or a large business and no matter where you are in your industry's value chain. The first way is to make a lot of money by selling a lot of product and making a lot of people happy. The second way is by being more efficient than your competitors.

So far, I haven't told you much about efficiency. I will in this chapter.

I should begin by saying that being more efficient means producing more product with fewer productive inputs. Take steel, for example. If you can manufacture it with less labor and energy consumption, you stand to save a lot of money. Efficiencies aren't always technological, though. In this chapter, I'll be focusing on other kinds of efficiencies—especially the kind that can help you run a customer satisfaction business downstream in the value chain.

It may seem odd that I'm talking about efficiency in a book devoted to customer satisfaction. But think about it: Customer satisfaction involves a *cost*—typically, about 5 percent of your gross sales. If you can make up that cost through efficiency, then satisfying the customer costs you nothing!

Impossible!!!

—Bob Tasca Sr.

When the German Ford dealers come here to my dealership seminars, they don't believe their eyes. They walk in, take a look around, and then they say, "Impossible! This can't be the real store! You can't possibly do this much business out of this tiny little space. Where's the real store?"

When they see our service area, they really go ballistic. "You can't possibly do service for three thousand new car sales out of only nine service bays. In Germany, we need fifty-four bays to do that much work!"

They just can't believe that we're six times more efficient than they are.

MORAL:

Customer satisfaction can pay for itself—if you're efficient enough.

How do you gain efficiency? The entire answer can be found in one simple rule: *Bricks and mortar don't sell product; people do.* Now, there's nothing unique about this expression. We didn't invent it; it's almost a business cliché. How we put it into practice, however, is—I believe—unique.

The Bottom Line

Never worry about the bottom line.

—THE FIFTH COMMANDMENT FOR CUSTOMER SATISFACTION

Do not let your left hand know what your right hand is doing.

—MATTHEW 6:3

Think about a stylized profit-and-loss statement for a moment. It begins with sales—what the British like to call the *top line*. After the cost to make or buy the product, practically everything else is expense. Expenses are related either to selling product or to overhead. Think of selling expenses as being everything that helps satisfy the customer—including service, of course. Subtract the everything else from the top line, and you get net profits—the *bottom line*. This being the case, the key to business efficiency is to reduce overhead to a minimum and put the savings into selling expenses, especially into customer satisfaction. Then in the long run you'll make both the top line and the bottom line happen.

Remember the Fifth Commandment for Customer Satisfaction: *Never worry about the bottom line*? Well, that's true—but only when you're dealing with your customers. That commandment really means, never think about the cost to *satisfy a customer*; just do it. The rest of the time, you must manage your costs very closely, because overhead cost savings must help *pay* for satisfying the customer.

Put another way, you satisfy your customers with your right hand and manage the bottom line with your left hand—and never let either hand know what the other is doing, so that you're not tempted to cheat.

The best way I know of to manage the bottom line is to begin with physical plant. As I've already told you, I just love small, neat, clean, *efficient* stores. As a customer, I love them because they can be so pleasant to shop in. As a businessman, I love them because smallness relative to sales volume minimizes many overheads.

Of course, any business facility can be small, clean, and efficient—not just retail stores. No matter what business you're in, having small and efficient facilities can give you an operating cost advantage over the competitor who's careless about overheads. You can then spend the difference on satisfying your customers.

Let me give you an example of physical plant specs from my industry. As far as we can tell, the average new car dealership occupies a physical plant of about twenty-five thousand square feet. It sells about six hundred new car units annually.

If the car manufacturers had their druthers, they'd set square footage considerably above twenty-five thousand; they'd like their average dealership to be closer to forty thousand square feet. Many dealerships are still substandard, though. At our Lincoln-Mercury store, we're *really* substandard. In fact, as I've already told you, our store was originally designed to sell and service only 390 new cars annually. We have only thirteen thousand square feet, yet we've sold as many as 3,664 new cars in one year out of that facility.

Right now, we only sell about half that many; the Rhode Island market hasn't recovered from the last recession. I guess you could say we're only running at half throttle. Nevertheless, we're still the most efficient new-car dealer in the country—probably in the world. Our efficiency starts with the tiny physical plant.

A look at "Bricks and Mortar Efficiency" pretty much tells the story. We use far less space to sell and service product than our competitors do. In fact, if we operated with the physical plant efficiency of the average dealership, we'd need about eighty thousand square feet to do what we now do in thirteen. There's no way on earth we could be over three times as profitable as the average dealership if we had that kind of plant liability. Yes, small *is* beautiful.

Bricks and Mortar Efficiency

Characteristic	1994	
	Tasca Lincoln-Mercury	Industry Average
Number of service bays per technician	0.45	1.6
Annual sales per square foot	$5,250.00	$761.00
Annual new and used car unit sales per 1,000 square feet	217	44
Annual service and parts sales per service bay	$773,156.77	$152,148.62
Annual service work orders done per bay	4,054.33	587.19

(Sources: Tasca Lincoln-Mercury and the NADA annual dealership survey.)

Small can be beautiful in your business, too. Tasca Lincoln-Mercury is living proof that you don't have to mortgage your future to the banks to run a successful business today. If you can keep your physical plant small and efficient, you can do better than many larger businesses and chains. We have mega-dealers in our trading area, yet we have no trouble competing against them. The formula is simple: Keep your overheads low by using small, efficient physical plants and invest the savings in customer satisfaction.

Bricks and Mortar Don't Sell Product; People Do

At Tasca, we also gain an efficiency advantage over our competitors through the productivity of our people. In a given metropolitan area, every dealership has to pay pretty much the same costs to employ a worker—base pay, taxes, insurances, benefits. What separates us from our competitors is the quantity of work our people produce. "People Efficiency" shows you the difference.

People Efficiency

Characteristic	1994 Tasca Lincoln-Mercury	Industry Average
Annual total sales per employee	$669,066.00	$452,823.00
Annual new and used car sales per salesperson	$3,149,125.00	$1,900,549.00
Annual new and used car unit sales per salesperson	166.53	126.25
Annual service and parts sales per working technician	$248,514.00	$243,437.00
Annual work orders done per working technician	1303.20	939.50
Number of inventory turnovers per year	6.3	4.4

(Sources: Tasca Lincoln-Mercury and the NADA annual dealership survey.)

As you can see, my co-workers produce far more work that has value than my competitors' workers do. There's only one area where we don't significantly outperform the average dealership, and that's in service sales dollars per technician. A Tasca technician completes 39 percent more work orders, but earns the dealership very little more in sales per year. Why? We don't pay our technicians to sell extra parts—and the numbers prove it. (Remember, that's one of the ways we satisfy customers—by never charging them for something they don't need.)

You may also wonder why our salespeople generate so many more car sales dollars per worker. It's not because they sell Lincolns, a higher-priced model, I can assure you. Everybody's sales of cream-of-the-crop luxury cars are off. No, it's because we let our salespeople resell only the best trade-ins; the rest we immediately wholesale, and those sales don't appear in our numbers. We don't want to sell anything that won't make our customers happy.

What's the implication of all this people efficiency my co-workers generate? Well, if my co-workers had only the productivity of the average dealership, we'd need to employ at least 25 percent more technicians and nearly 50 percent more salespeople than we do presently. And the extra cost that reflects would make it hard to incur the cost of satisfying the customer. Very soon, our customer satisfaction–based business would start to unwind.

It may seem strange to you, but we employ so few people *because* we run a customer satisfaction business—not *in spite of* running such a business. This runs counter to conventional thinking about customer service businesses. The conventional thinking is that you have to hire more people per unit of business if you want to satisfy your customers. Well, we don't do that.

Remember that we don't have a customer service department or customer representatives. That's a big people overhead savings. At our dealerships, satisfying the customer is everybody's job, so we don't need to employ additional specialists. We also don't employ assistant sales managers to whom salespeople must go for a sales authorization. Our salespeople don't have to horse-trade with an assistant manager; all they have to do is satisfy the customer. We eliminate another level of management in our service department, where we use working lead technicians instead of nonworking supervisors. We save all of these people overheads, and then we invest them in customer satisfaction.

What I've described here might be called the *miracle of customer satisfaction*—how fewer people can satisfy more customers. So far, I've given you two efficencies that can allow you to run a business more effectively: bricks and mortar, and people. There is, however, a third form of efficiency.

The Store as an Efficient Engine—Not a Building

A store is not a building—it's an economic engine. How well you "mind the store" determines how efficiently your economic engine runs. Minding the store is, of course, an expression that means "managing the business," so I'm really talking here about all businesses that serve large numbers of customers.

How can you make your economic engine run better than your competitor's? All engines perform work, whether they're internal combustion engines, steam engines, or economic engines. My business engines are designed to produce customer satisfaction; that's the kind of work they do. Now, all engines take in some kind of fuel, and they convert that fuel into work. In most cases, the fuel is potential buyers. Some of them get converted into new customers; some of them don't buy at all. Just as all engines waste some of their fuel's energy, you'll waste some potential buyers. If you want an efficient business engine, though, you don't want to waste many potential buyers. That's why you have to satisfy the customer—from the moment she first has contact with you.

All business engines go through two operations to produce their results: They sell customers and they make a product— whether the product is a tangible thing or a service or a combination. The only two questions are, "Does your business engine run on a closed-cycle or an open-cycle principle?" and "Which operation comes first in your business?"

Let's get into this cycle issue in more detail. How many of your customers—the real fuel for your engine—does your business *recycle?* How many of the people you sold for the first time buy from you again? How many become customers for life? Does your business recycle customers or do your customers just go out the exhaust pipe? Obviously, the more customers you can recycle, the more efficient your business engine will be. Remember, the easiest customer to sell is the one you've already sold *and satisfied.* This, in turn, suggests something about the order in which your business engine should perform its work: first people selling and then product making.

Why is this the right order? Because the purpose of the product is to satisfy customers. In our business, we sell people first. Then we make a product to suit the customer—not ourselves. We happen to make automotive services. That's our product. An automobile is just the raw material that we use. Actually, we make automotive services in a special way. Our product is designed to do just two things: satisfy the customer and lead the customer back to the sales door. That way, we create a closed-cycle business engine; we continually reuse many of the same customers. We sell them and satisfy them, over and over again. That's far more efficient than starting with fresh, cold customers who don't yet trust you.

Notice how everybody's job becomes easier when everybody's job is to satisfy the customer. Salespeople have a much easier job, because they resell so many customers. In fact, the entire business needs much less "new customer fuel" for its engine. Service technicians and people fixers both have easier jobs, because a satisfied customer is likely to trade more often: The service department will repair fewer older products—which are harder to fix and harder to satisfy the customer with.

To complete an efficient business engine, though, you must supercharge it. The way you do that is by paying your people to satisfy customers, not make the business gross profits. Then your co-workers both cooperate and compete—all to satisfy, and ultimately sell, more customers. The entire engine now performs like one in a race car. That's business efficiency.

Supercharge Your Business

You may be wondering how generally these principles apply. Are they just for traditional retail stores? Of course not. How do you think L.L. Bean and Lands' End got to be so successful? They deliver product that suits the taker, not the maker; they determine how to sell the product before they "make" it. Their customer service is legendary.

For another example of business efficiency, look at Wal-Mart. One of the reasons that Sam Walton got to be so successful was that he understood business efficiency; he built a huge business success story based on small, efficient stores. I knew Sam Walton pretty well. In fact, he once asked me to take a look at one of his stores; it was doing much less well than some of his others. It was immediately obvious to me why that was the case; the store wasn't bright enough, and it looked cluttered. The problem resided in the details;

they all added up to *dingy*. He hadn't seen it; I guess he was too close to the problem that time. Once I pointed it out to him, he changed the store, and it took off.

The Efficient Business Engine

- **There are only two ways to make a lot of money.** Either by making a lot of people happy or by being more efficient than your competitors.
- **Business efficiency can pay for the costs of customer satisfaction.**
- **Customer satisfaction can become an investment with real future payoffs.** If you can use customer satisfaction expense to increase customer loyalty and your business reputation, it becomes an investment rather than a cost.
- **Bricks and mortar don't sell product; people do.** Use your overhead savings from a small, efficient physical plant to pay your customer satisfaction costs.
- **Never let your left hand know what your right hand is doing.** Never worry about the bottom line when you're satisfying the customer; the rest of the time, always worry about it—and keep the two concerns separate.
- **Business efficiency comes from both overhead efficiency and people efficiency.** Overhead efficiency is gained from sticking with small facilities; people efficiency comes from making it everyone's job to satisfy the customer—you save on wasteful middle management.
- **An efficient business engine recycles its fuel.** A business engine's fuel is its customers.
- **An efficient business engine sells people first, then makes a product to suit the taker, not the maker.** Get the content and price combination right first, then make the product to suit your customer's preferences for each.
- **Supercharge your business engine for even greater efficiency.** Pay your co-workers to satisfy customers, not to make you a gross profit; now, your co-workers will both cooperate and compete among themselves—all to sell and satisfy more customers.

15

Don't Just *Satisfy* Your Customer, Make Her Happy

What Have We Really Been Measuring?

What does it really mean when we say that we have a satisfied customer? Well, it seems to me that what we've been measuring is the absence of some forms of *dis*satisfaction. By this definition, a satisfied customer is one who isn't *dis*satisfied. At least, he doesn't express dissatisfaction on one of the standard surveys.

The customer satisfaction surveys tend to focus on things gone wrong. In other words, they ask customers to report on a factual basis. This all seems perfectly reasonable. Did the product itself fail in initial quality or use, and if so, what part of it failed? Did the business that sold you the product fail to do certain things? If the answer is no to both these sets of questions, we presume the customer is satisfied. Now there's sense in this approach, and there's also something wrong with it. Let's deal with the sense first.

Until fairly recently, many American businesses—both manufacturers and retailers—didn't do very well when measured against these standards. They didn't always operate to provide *basic* customer satisfaction. So concentrating on reducing things gone wrong was the place to begin. Lately, though, we've started to see the inadequacies of this basic approach.

Satisfaction is a feeling and an attitude—not an objective measurement of anything. People live in *relationship* to many of the products they buy. Just consider how much time in your life you spend with your automobile—or your stereo set or your kitchen appliances. In relationships, people don't normally enter the things gone wrong in a ledger. Do you count the things gone wrong in your marriage as the way of judging how good it is? Hopefully not. Hence, when we obsessively measure things gone wrong with a product, we're missing the larger point.

First of all, everybody doesn't look for the same things in a given product or relationship. People's needs and wants vary with their circumstances—social, economic, life stage, and so on. In my business, for example, we may fail to satisfy a busy professional if we don't write up her service order within four minutes of her arrival. On the other hand, we may fail to satisfy a lonely housewife if we *do* write the order up within four minutes. She may not really like it that we *did* fix her car right the first time; she may enjoy the visits and the attention she gets.

Do you know the biggest reason we lose loyal customers at Lincoln-Mercury? They become bored with the product. They're perfectly satisfied with us, but the product no longer excites them; they want to try something else.

Second, we don't measure *pleasure* when we measure satisfaction; all that we measure is the absence of *pain*. Do you love your spouse only because she or he is a low-maintenance person? Presumably, you love her, because you thoroughly enjoy her. It's the same way with many products. Do you enjoy a product that costs you only a little to maintain but does nothing else *for* you? Isn't there something missing in that relationship?

The Difference between Satisfaction and Happiness

Consumers are sending an important signal to automotive manufacturers. The message is that there is considerable opportunity for product enhancements to make cars and trucks more appealing to own and operate.

—J. D. POWER III

If a vehicle is going to be more than a "toaster with wheels," it needs to do some things that delight the customer.

—DARREL EDWARDS, STRATEGIC
VISION, INC.

There is a difference between mere satisfaction and happiness then. Satisfaction is the feeling we've been treated fairly. In regard to products, happiness is the joy of ownership.

As an example, let's say you bought a new car from me. Let's also say that, after you bought it, you just didn't like the car. I've tried to satisfy you by handling your every objection, but you still just don't like the product. I really don't know why; maybe you don't either. Ultimately, I can satisfy you: I can give you your money back. You will then feel that you've been *fairly treated*. I did everything I could for you. But will you feel happy about the experience? No. You wanted to experience *the joy of new*, and you didn't receive it.

Can we pledge to make you happy? No. From my earliest days in business, I've always tried to go beyond satisfying my customers; I've tried to make them happy. I can't *promise* it, but I sure can try—via the myriad ways I've described so far in these pages: extraordinary service hours, blueprinting, and a no-hassle sales experience.

Can *you* run a business on the happiness principle—the next frontier beyond customer satisfaction? I believe you can. Can you do it even if you happen to make and sell a product that isn't as potentially exciting as an automobile? Yes. It doesn't matter what business you run or where you are in the value chain. You see, no matter what kind of business you run, you sell people. That means you have the opportunity to make your "customers" satisfied, or even better, happy. That's true even if you're a dentist or someone else selling a good that has a "bad" in it.

I predict that the happiness principle will begin to complement, not replace, customer satisfaction as the new goal for business in America. There's even a good chance it will happen on a broad basis first in the auto industry—for reasons I'm about to explain.

What We Should Be Measuring

To run a business based on the happiness principle, you have to be able to *measure* happiness. For the automobile industry, this is already beginning to happen.

How do you measure a customer's happiness with a product such as an automobile? You start by defining something that might be called *Automotive Performance, Execution, and Layout* (APEAL) or *Total Quality Index* (TQI). That's what J.D. Power and Strategic Vision have named their customer happiness measurement programs, respectively. The focus is on the customer's experience of ownership and away from things gone wrong with the car.

For Strategic Vision, *quality* means the quality of the customer's total car-ownership experience. *Total* means taking into account both the absence of pain and the presence of pleasure. The pleasures score as positives, and the pains score as negatives in computing the index. When you compute the TQI number, you've measured the customer's happiness with the product.

Let's consider what the customer does when she rates her new automobile. She begins with her expectations of the *joy of new*. Then she judges the ability of the car to meet or exceed those expectations. She may even become delighted to find that the automobile is surprising her by creating new expectations that she hadn't looked to find pleasure in experiencing.

How does this differ from measuring things gone wrong and things done right? Well, as I've already pointed out, different people respond with different intensities of emotion to different things in a product. Everybody's pleasure points and pain points are not the same. Different types of people respond differently to the identical thing gone wrong, or thing done right. Some people find pleasure in contemplating the craftsmanship of a Rolls-Royce. Some people take pleasure in taking their high-performance car into the shop to be tuned up; reliability in this case isn't a positive attribute. Such a person would find a trouble-free car boring.

Different people purchase different cars for just such reasons. That's why we don't all drive Model T Fords or Russian Ladas. Also, different cars get judged on different pleasure and pain criteria by the same type of customer. We all expect different things out of different products. In all cases, people's expectations—their beliefs about what the brand should and shouldn't do—form the basis of their emotional responses to the actual experience of ownership.

While all of this sounds terribly complex, and it is, a conceptual measure such as APEAL or TQI has the power to reduce all of these variables down to a single number. These measures could, in fact, work as the psychological equivalent to the economic price of a product.

What can all of this mean for the car manufacturer and car retailer? First of all, it may in the future revolutionize the way customers think about quality itself. Notice what's happening here. Quality has been redefined into terms of *emotional response to expectations*, whereas until now it has been defined as *rational response to functionality*. What might that do for the ratings of automobiles?

Well, one example that has recently come to the attention of the auto journalists involves a new small car from Chrysler called the Neon. The Neon represents both what's great and what's not so great about Chrysler. Bob Lutz is a great car man, and the Neon is an innovative design. It's not perfected, however, and Chrysler simply doesn't have the design or build quality that we've achieved at Ford. So, the Neon scores low on build quality and high on NVH (noise, vibration, and harshness). That triggers a low rating on initial quality from J.D. Power.

However, the Neon also possesses some "surprise and delight" design attributes that excite its owners, and it's cute. Some people really love their Neons. When Strategic Vision scores the car on a TQI basis, lo and behold! It jumps from the bottom of the pack to the top. When J.D. Power scores the car on APEAL, it's second only to a Golf GTI! It seems to me that an APEAL or TQI sort of rating system for automobiles will reward manufacturers for their design brilliance as well as for their build quality—and that's a long overdue thing. It will help distinguish products such as Ford's new Taurus-Sables from the design also-rans.

I'm excited about this way of measuring people's responses to automotive products, because it recognizes the happiness factor present in each car. Why should a terrific car that owners love be at the bottom of the ratings strictly because of one minor initial quality or reliability failing? It seems to me that measuring the happiness factor for automobiles opens up a whole new opportunity for successful competition—for makers and sellers alike. And, it should be possible to do the same thing in other industries as well.

Managing for Customer Happiness

When you can measure happiness, you can manage on it. In our businesses, we've always intuitively tried to make the customer happy. In the future, it may become possible to practice managing for customer happiness in a systematic way. To do so, people in the industry must first come to better understand customers' needs. We all have a variety of needs that our vehicles satisfy—and sometimes give us pleasure in fulfilling. Perhaps cars and sport utility vehicles (SUVs) need to be classified by the needs they fill and how well they do it, rather than by their size and interior volumes. Each vehicle's TQI rating will then become an important marketing tool for the maker and the dealer—as important, or more so, than the economic price. Car makers will design cars to be more fun. Both manufacturers and retailers will receive fairer rewards for helping create customer happiness.

Different types of people purchase different types of vehicles. We dealers must become better at understanding our customers' needs and help them find the product that will best suit them—treating the customer as custom. I've always done that for my customers. But it must become a more common practice. That means, in turn, that we dealers should become more influential within the companies whose products we sell. We must become the experts on real human needs for our industry. We must better represent those needs to our suppliers. Once again, the wonderful partnership that I've had with the Ford Motor Company for more than fifty years must become more typical, not an aberration.

Happiness Principles

- **Individual product needs vary.** Our needs are based on our social and economic circumstances, our life stage, our personal values, and our self image. Happiness is created when our expectations about a product are met or exceeded.

- **When customers rate products, their responses are shaped by their expectations.** People rate products on the basis of the product's ability to meet or exceed expectations and on the product's ability to create new expectations as it delights them.
- **Measuring things gone wrong will never determine product happiness.** Even when we also measure things done right, that is not enough. We need to measure the emotional response to both things gone wrong and things done right—in relation to expectations.
- **Measuring customer happiness is the first step to delivering it.** Unless you can measure it, you cannot manage for it.
- **Customer satisfaction can be promised; customer happiness can't.** Satisfaction is largely based on the fairness principle. Happiness, though, is beyond your control. Still, you should always strive to delight your customers.
- **Making customers happy involves understanding your customer.** Matching the product to the type of person who is your customer becomes crucial in a customer happiness business. Treat your customer as custom.

(Partial source: Strategic Visions, Inc.)

Leadership:
A Constant Challenge, Not a Reward

Your Employees Will Do What They See You Do

The greatest leadership failings derive from the belief that as a leader you can do things you forbid your employees to do. That sets a behavioral double standard, and it will always boomerang. It's particularly disastrous in a customer satisfaction business. As I've pointed out, if you personally gouge customers to increase your business profits, you can hardly expect your people to treat your customers fairly. If you practice favoritism with some customers, your employees will do the same. If you favor certain employees, the rest will come to hate you and your favorites. Remember, leadership in a customer satisfaction business means practicing absolute personal integrity; that's the only way to run a business where nobody has to lie.

The Monkey up the Flag Pole

—Bob Tasca Sr.

Back in the late 1950s when I was first becoming successful in business and had begun to run seminars for other Ford dealers, Charlie Beecham took me aside one day. Beecham, you'll remember, was a

colorful old-line Ford sales manager with rough manners but integrity
so fine it could cut like a knife. He said, "Kid, have you ever gone to the
zoo, and watched the monkeys? Sometimes, one of them will climb up
a flag pole. And, as he climbs the pole, the higher he goes the more his
you-know-what shows. As you go up the business flagpole, always
remember to keep your you-know-what clean."

I suspect that some business people fall into a trap in this
regard. They practice a double standard when they're low-level
managers, and they don't get caught at it. Pretty soon, the double
standard becomes a way of life. Then they get very high up the ladder, and their behaviors are exposed. They may be genuinely surprised by the fallout, because they'd been led to believe that the
gains yielded by practicing a double standard are leadership's nat-
ural reward. They're not.

You see, leadership is never a reward. Reward is always backward looking; it gives you something for what you achieved in the
past. Good managers *do* earn rewards for solving problems. Great
leaders never do.

Nothing can destroy a business like favoritism. It's a particular
problem for family businesses, and yes, I've had to deal with it. My
three sons and my daughter have all been involved in our businesses.
(Right now, my daughter is raising a family, but someday she'll be
back in the business, I hope.) My three sons have never even imagined doing anything else. I know that many family businesses get into
trouble when the owner's offspring grow up apart from the business,
then try to enter the business after college. Often, they have what I
call "head knowledge" but the business knowledge is lacking. In such
cases, giving these young people positions of responsibility causes a
lot of resentment, and sometimes some awfully bad business decisions get made while they're learning the ropes.

What Did You *Earn* Today?

—David Tasca

When we were growing up, whenever any of us would ask Dad for
something, like a bicycle, he'd reply: "What did you earn today?" Then

he'd give us a job so we could earn what we wanted. We all started off in the business early in life. After school, the Tasca Ford parts van would pick us up. Other kids went home; we went to work at the business. Each one of us learned everything, from the bottom up. We did that right through college.

In our family business, the kids got involved early. While they were in grade school, they began learning everything about the dealership. They were sweeping floors in the Parts and Service departments and learning to tinker with car engines before they were eight years old. From the beginning, I made it clear that they'd have to earn their success in the family business the same way I did—by working harder than anybody else. I guess it worked, because they're all still with me. Each one now runs a part of the business I once ran alone; each has come to represent a part of *me* as a businessman, you might say.

Today, my sons pretty much run our businesses. I spend most of my time working to help the Ford Motor Company with selling product, product design, and quality.

An Evening at the Racetrack

—Bob Tasca Jr.

When I was eleven years old and Carl was nine, we'd already built up our own street-class drag racers. We both had Fairlanes with pretty powerful V8 engines in them. They were fast cars. One night that summer, we found a way to enter the drag races at a local track. So, there we were, lined up right next to one another, powerful engines throbbing. Carl was still so short that when he would dump the clutch and burn rubber, he could barely peer over the hood to see where he was going. I looked over to my left at Carl lined up next to me. I could just barely see his head. He looked scared; probably I did too. We were both illegal as hell. Then, I looked to my right to see who else I was running against, and there was Dad! Do you know what the worst part of it was? He beat me!

A lot of people ask me about how you transfer authority and responsibility to others as your business grows. Too many business people try to keep total control for too long. It's pretty much the same whether you delegate authority and responsibility to family members or to other co-workers. I guess the most important thing is trust; if you run a business based on integrity in customer satisfaction, ultimately you have to completely trust your people. You need to let go. You need to give your people the opportunity to make their own mistakes. Otherwise, how will they ever learn?

Take This Check and Invest It

—Carl Tasca

When Dad sold the Ford dealership in 1971, there was going to be a closing on the deal down at Industrial National Bank in Providence. The dealer who was buying the franchise was going to be there with his people, a manager from Ford was going to be there, and of course, a banker. Dad told us we were coming with him—Bob Junior and I. I was eighteen years old at the time; Bob Junior was twenty; this was a big thing for us. He also took Aunt Jean along—an amazing woman who rose to the top of the CPA profession in the state without ever even going to college. I'd always been interested in finance—the numbers part of a business—and I was beginning to handle some of that part of our business. Needless to say, I was excited about going along.

We all sat around in a big conference room for a while, just talking, until the Ford manager suggested that we get down to business. Then he said, "Get those kids out of here."

Slowly Dad got up from the table. He snapped his briefcase shut, and he started to walk out of the room. "Where are you going?" the Ford guy said, sounding irritated. "We've got to get this thing over with."

"The deal's off," Dad said, as he strode toward the door. "If my kids aren't here, I'm not here." "Let's go," he said to us.

Well, the guy from Ford nearly had a heart attack. "Stop! Wait! It's okay if the kids stay in, I guess. We can't lose this deal now!"

You see, the deal was for $1,771,000; that was a lot for an auto franchise back in 1971. It was the second largest Ford dealership in the world, and the sale was critical. It had to go through, right away.

Ford was very concerned about this sale. I think the guy saw his career going up in smoke right in front of his eyes. Dad stopped and looked back at him. He paused for a moment. The Ford guy's heart must have been pounding. "Okay, we go ahead," he said.

About twenty minutes later, everything was signed, sealed, and delivered. The banker handed Dad a cashier's check for $1,771,000. Do you know what Dad did? He handed it to *me*—an eighteen-year-old kid, remember—and he said to me, "Here, take this check and invest it."

I watched the guy from Ford, and I thought he was going to drop his trousers.

That was twenty-four years ago now. You know what? Dad has never once asked me what I did with that money or what it's now worth. Not once. Of course, it's worth a lot more now. He trusted me. That's how he's always been, with all four of us. When he gives us responsibility, he really gives it. No questions asked. That was also how he raised us; when we were kids, he never told us to leave the room because adults were present. That's how he treats his German shepherds today; they never get sent out if people come over to visit. I'd like to think that he hasn't raised bad dogs or bad kids because of it.

Managers Solve Problems; Leaders Prevent Them

Many business people seem to lose sight of the difference between managing and leading. The difference is really very simple, and it's critical to running a customer happiness business. You see, managers are hired for only one reason: to solve problems. In a perfect world, one without any problems, managers would have nothing to do. We all live in a world, however, where problems are always happening; problems are the penalty for living. In a business where you're trying to satisfy the customer, and if possible make her happy, managers are critical; they're the people who must solve your customer's problems.

Remember what defines a business problem: something that adversely affects, or will affect, your customer. If it doesn't have present or future adverse effect on your customers, it's not a business problem. Too many business people waste time on things that aren't their business's real problems. They don't solve problems; they avoid them.

Leaders, however, don't solve problems; they *prevent* them. That means they're essentially forward looking; they must be able to see today how some present problem can be eliminated in the future. The best way to solve a problem, of course, is to eliminate it so it can't happen again. Managers, on the other hand, are backward looking; they must collect the facts necessary to solve existing problems—all of which began in the past. We need both sorts of people, but leaders are unique and very hard to find.

A Constant Challenge—Not a Reward

Back in 1961, I wrote a short piece on leadership (see "Leadership Principles"). I was only thirty-five years old at the time, but I don't think I was too far off. It began with this sentence: "Leadership is not a *reward*; it is a constant *challenge*." I went on to characterize leadership as consisting of *action* generating a constant forward motion—not self-gratification.

In the automobile business, for example, the design of new product is a critical activity. In fact, it's really the core of the auto manufacturer's business. (*Auto manufacturer* is actually a misnomer; "auto designer" is a better fit. Everything besides design, including production, can theoretically be farmed out.) Now, when you talk about auto design, two things are important—reach and stretch. Stretch is backward; stretch ties a current design into the brand's themes from the past. Stretch is what you do to an older design to prolong its life in the market. Reach, on the other hand, is future oriented. Reach is a measure of a new design's future integrity in the marketplace.

Designing for reach is betting on the come, not on the came. Finance people like to bet on the came; it seems so much safer and smaller a bet. But in actuality, it's rapidly becoming the most dangerous bet you can make. If you decide to stretch an existing product, you run the risk of being as much as ten years behind the market five years from now. That's why finance people have trouble leading car companies—and any other companies that are in a fast-changing market environment.

The goal for good automotive product design should be five

years' future reach. That is, a new product should be designed today to have appeal in the marketplace five years from now. Coming up with products with five years' reach is one of the toughest things to do in the auto business. It means you have to know today what will be hot in the market five years from now. It involves a real feel for the market and a sense of vision. In other words, it requires real product leadership ability.

In the auto business today, five years' reach will buy you a product that is still design competitive two years after it's entered the market. That assumes you're able to get the new product to market in a three-year design cycle time. In the 1970s and 1980s, it used to take Detroit six to seven years to cycle a new product. Now we're back down to three—where we used to be before government regulations made the design cycles much more complicated. We're just about competitive with the Japanese. Soon, we'll be down to two years.

Nobody can predict what completed designs will sell seven years out—that's why reducing the design cycle time has been so important. Now that everybody's getting down under three years, design has become a much more competitive matter. Great leadership in the auto manufacturers' core activity will matter even more in the future. Nobody will be competitive without innovative designs that have reach.

The current chairman of the Ford Motor Company, Alex Trotman, is a man who came to his job with a real sense of vision. I should know; I've worked with Alex since the early 1970s; in the 1980s, we worked together on the idea for Ford's current product design vision. That vision's now becoming a reality in the form of the Ford 2000 plan.

You might say that our design strategy had pretty good reach; about twenty years after we first conceived it, it'll be put fully into place, and it'll be very competitive. I don't think this sort of product instinct can be taught. Does that mean that real leadership can't be learned? No. But it does mean that leaders who don't possess the instinct have to have the good sense to hire people who do, who can advise them. It's just an application of the personnel rule: Hire people who are smarter than you.

At the inception of Ford 2000, back in the early 1980s, everybody thought we were crazy—that it couldn't be done. After all, the design cycle time was stretching out to as much as seven years; it wasn't going down—it was going up. How could you design new platforms on a three-year cycle when it actually took you seven? Well, starting with Team Taurus, which I was a part of, we began to learn how to design cars in a whole new way. Now we're making the company joke of the early 1980s into the future of the auto industry. Do you know the one thing I hope and pray for most? That I'll live long enough to see it all happen.

What we're doing at Ford is really just an example of my basic rules for making a lot of money in any business. First and foremost, *sell a lot of product*—in this case, by providing our customers with exciting and innovative new car designs on a shorter design cycle to correspond with their shorter trading cycle under the Pre-Trade Plan. With the shorter design cycle, no Pre-Trade customer will ever have to repurchase what is essentially the same product more than once.

Second, *be more efficient than your competitors*. The shorter your design cycle, everything else being equal, the more efficient you are. Last, *satisfy the customer; if possible, make her happy*. We'll be doing that to a degree and level never before imagined.

Leadership, then, involves future reach. As I wrote back in 1961, it involves *vitality*. Vitality is constant forward motion, with vigor—motion faster than all competitors. Myself, I'm a perpetual motion machine. I'm always working on what I'm going to do next. When I decide what it is, I very rarely fail to make it happen. I make it happen by betting on the come. You'll never succeed as a leader in any business unless you see the future as a constant challenge to be met with vitality.

Remember, *the best never rest*. Leadership involves progress— the belief that today's excellence will never be good enough for tomorrow.

The Phillips Head Screwdriver

—David Tasca

One of the things I remember most about Dad when I was growing up was that when he came home from work, no matter what time it was, he'd probably be honking the horn for me. That meant I needed to run outside to him with a Phillips head screwdriver and help him adjust the headlights on whatever car he was driving. It might be midnight in a snowstorm, but I'd be out there turning that screwdriver while he yelled, "up a little!" or down a little!"—judging the setting of the headlights shining against the garage door. They had to be *perfect.* That's how he was. It was the same way with the sprinkling system for the lawn. We might spend a whole Sunday working together to get the sprinkler heads perfect. Today, I'm the same way. If one new car out of three hundred on our lot is an inch out of line, I have to go out and fix it so the line is perfect.

The other thing I remember is that when it really mattered for us, Dad was always there. As a kid, I loved athletics. Despite his busy work life, Dad always took time out to attend my games; in fact, he took the time to coach some of the teams I was on as well.

Leadership also involves attracting followers and building *followership.* Followership involves imitation—doing what you see a leader do—because not everybody can anticipate the market's future direction or duplicate the actions of a leader.

Leadership involves *good citizenship.* Find some nonprofit organization in your local community—a church or a school, for instance—and adopt it for your support. I've done that both with a local college and a local parochial school. (Any profits I make from this book will go to St. Rocco's School in Johnston, Rhode Island.)Finally, leadership really involves people—understanding them, knowing their needs and wants, helping them achieve personal satisfaction. That's why I always sell people, not products— why I hire co-workers, not employees.

Tasca University

When Ford gave me a party to celebrate my fiftieth anniversary with the company, Red Poling, who was chairman then, got up and announced that over the years "Tasca University," as he called it, had trained 165,000 people for Ford. I don't know how he came up with that number; but knowing Red, I'm sure he found some way to get an accurate count. That's a lot of people who've been influenced by our business practices.

Of course, Tasca University doesn't exist in bricks and mortar; I didn't go out and endow a university. What I did do, starting with that first seminar I ran for Charlie Beecham, was train two generations of Ford dealership personnel in my business and leadership practices. Over the years, I've given a lot of time to this endeavor.

Even now, my people and I give up a couple days a month to run Tasca University. Why do I do it? Well, Ford has been very good to me over the years, and I want to pay some of that back. I don't look for a reward for the leadership I've provided Ford. I look at the constant challenge facing Ford and my fellow dealers, and I feel I can still make a contribution.

At Tasca University, we also run training sessions to teach Ford assembly plant people something of what we've learned over the years about blueprinting cars. This is something I'm a fanatic about, and it's rubbed off on my people. We don't teach Ford people how to build cars; it would be arrogant to even think we could do that. We do teach some of the methods we use to boost the quality level of the product being built.

Most of all, I think we teach some Ford managers new attitudes about perfection in building automobiles. We're closer to the customer, and we know what it takes to really satisfy him. Do you know what I've seen happen in the past? I've seen some Ford managers come to us and really get converted about quality. They've gone back to their plants and revolutionized them.

Paul Nolan came to us back in the days when his plant built the Ford Fairmont/Mercury Zephyr; it was, quite frankly, a pretty terrible car. When he saw what we did with a Fairmont/Zephyr to improve its quality, he was amazed. He went back and began transforming his assembly plant. He ordered new jigs and fixtures and bought new dies. Working together, his people turned a poor car into a car that had more quality in it than it seemed possible to build. After that, he went on to run our Wixom plant, and he had a lot to do with the Lincoln's ranking among the best-quality cars in the world.

That's what attitude can do, when you have high standards. That's what we've tried to accomplish at Tasca University—changing attitude and setting high standards. It's all part of leadership defined as eliminating problems before they even have a chance to happen.

Wealthy, Honest, Honorable

I believe there is a progression in the lives of most business people. Some of us find ways to become wealthy. When we do, we get concerned about being honest—honest enough to deserve and keep our wealth. If we live long enough to become honest, we may also become _honorable_—that is, recognized by the people in our community. I've pretty much followed that path—except for one thing. I've _always_ behaved honestly in getting wealth; I've always tried to satisfy my customers—no matter what it cost, even early on when I was trying very hard to become wealthy.

I've succeeded long enough now, while at the same time maintaining a high standard of integrity, that my family and its name are being recognized—where I live, and in the Ford Motor Company. We're being recognized—_and_ we're give something back in return for the help our customers and friends have given us. I want that to continue into the third generation in our family businesses; nothing concerns me more.

In the final analysis, there may _be_ one exception to the rule that "leadership is a constant challenge, not a reward." The exception? Well, if there's any reward to leadership, it's _honor_.

Honor only comes when you've met the challenges, and triumphed over them, year after year. It doesn't come without cost; but to me, it's all been worth it.

It's what lies at the end of the journey.

Leadership Principles

- Leadership is not a _reward;_ it is a constant _challenge_.
- Leadership is _action,_ movement—not existence or self-gratification.
- Leadership is _vitality_—a constant forward motion with vigor, and being faster than all competitors.
- Leadership is _progress_, a firm conviction that today's excellence must be exceeded with tomorrow's dawn.
- Leadership is _attracting followers_, making others imitate, since they cannot anticipate or duplicate
- Leadership is _good citizenship_, entailing great responsibilities.

- Leadership is, after all, *people*—knowing them, understanding their needs and wants, helping them to attain satisfaction.

Last, "Success is not a destination, it is a journey."

—Bob Tasca Sr., 1961

Appendix A

Sales Standards

- Customers courteously acknowledged within two minutes of arrival and advised that a sales consultant is available on request.
- Advisory relationship established by knowledgeable sales consultant who listens to customers, identifies needs, and ensures needs are met.
- Test drive offered to all customers.
- Pleasant, nonpressured purchase experience and thorough explanation provided by sales consultant, sales management, and F&I personnel.
- Using a checklist, sales consultant delivers vehicle in perfect condition when promised.
- Customers contacted by sales consultant within one week after delivery to ensure total satisfaction.

Appendix B

Service Standards

1. Appointment available within one day of customer's requested service day.
2. Write-up begins within four minutes of arrival.
3. Service needs courteously identified, accurately recorded on Repair Order, and verified with customer.
4. Product serviced right on the first visit.
5. Service status provided within one minute of inquiry.
6. Product is ready at agreed-on time.
7. Thorough explanation of work done, coverage, and charges.